of

BIG I

Rebel Shavetail Edition

★ ★ ★

Autographed by the editor
for the members of the

Civil War Book Club

Bill Wiley

REMINISCENCES OF BIG I

Library of Congress
Catalog Card No. 56-7451

Manufactured in the U. S. A. by
McCowat-Mercer Press, Inc., Jackson, Tennessee

REMINISCENCES
OF
BIG I

By

LIEUT. WILLIAM NATHANIEL WOOD

Monticello Guard, Company "A", 19th Virginia Regiment
Confederate States of America

Edited by

BELL IRVIN WILEY

MᶜCOWAT-MERCER PRESS, INC., JACKSON, TENNESSEE

1956

CONTENTS

v

ILLUSTRATIONS

Facing Page 2

PICKETT'S CHARGE AT GETTYSBURG

GENERAL RICHARD B. GARNETT

LIEUT. WILLIAM N. WOOD

GENERAL ROBERT E. LEE ON TRAVELLER

GENERAL GEORGE E. PICKETT

GENERAL EPPA HUNTON

GENERAL P. G. T. BEAUREGARD

GENERAL J. E. B. STUART

THE CONRAD HOUSE, BATTLEFIELD OF FIRST MANASSAS

RUINS OF THE HENRY HOUSE, BATTLEFIELD OF
FIRST BULL RUN

OLD CAPITOL PRISON, WASHINGTON, D. C.

JOHNSON'S ISLAND PRISON

WILLIAM N. WOOD AND HIS WIFE,
NANNIE BULLOCK WOOD

INTRODUCTION

Pickett's charge at Gettysburg probably has been the theme of more writing than any other action of the Civil War. Common soldiers, nurses, surgeons, journalists, foreign observers, local residents and generals have all recounted their experiences and impressions. But relatively few company commanders who participated in that grand but futile assault have left a record of what they saw and did. Indeed, and especially on the Confederate side, the role of junior officers as told by themselves, constitutes a major gap in Civil War literature. Because of this fact, William Nathaniel Wood's reminiscences of Gettysburg and the dozen other major battles in which he participated is of considerably greater value than the usual memoir.

Wood was a lieutenant at Gettysburg and apparently still a "shave-tail" (though that term seems not to have been current in the Civil War). But he was in command of Company "A," Nineteenth Virginia Infantry, in the desperate charge that proved the highwater mark of Confederate arms. When he reached the rock fence atop Cemetery Ridge, after running a gauntlet of fire and lead, he stopped momentarily to survey the situation. His reaction was one of horror. "I . . . felt we were disgraced," he wrote some thirty years later. "Where were those who started in the charge? With one single exception I witnessed no cowardice, and yet we had not a skirmish line."

With his foes closing in rapidly about him, Wood did not tarry to ponder his plight, but turned and fled down the slope which he had recently ascended. Bullets peppered his course and riddled his clothing. One ball broke the skin and for a time he thought himself mortally wounded. But examination revealed that the hit was only a scratch.

The scene that he beheld on his retreat accounted for the thinness of the line at the end of the charge. And when on his return to the jump-off point, General Pickett took him by the hand and then turned aside to sob, "My brave men! My brave men," Wood "felt that after all we were not disgraced." Even so, he was troubled by a lingering disappointment, because, as he put it, "We had for the first time, failed to do what we attempted."

William Nathaniel Wood, known by his intimates as "Nat," was born near Earlysville, in Albermarle County, Virginia, November 16, 1839. He was one of twelve children —eleven boys and one girl—born to Charles Ezekiel and Martha (Thomas) Wood. Little is known of William's boyhood, but two letters written while in Confederate service and his war reminiscences indicate that he received a good education, though apparently he did not attend college.

When the war broke out, William, then in his twenty-first year, was working as a clerk in a Charlottesville dry-goods store. His reminiscences state that he joined the army on July 19, 1861, at Manassas, but Confederate records in the National Archives give the place and time of his enlistment as Charlottesville, July 9, 1861. One of his war letters shows that he worked in the store through July 18. Hence, it seems likely that he signed up for service in Charlottesville on July 9 and joined his unit at Manassas on July 19.

Wood began his service as a private in Company "A," Nineteenth Virginia Infantry. His company, known as the Monticello Guard, was organized at Charlottesville, and its roster included a number of University of Virginia students.

The Nineteenth Virginia was at First Manassas, but Wood's participation was only nominal, as he did not fire a shot during that engagement and he had no soldier equipment except a hat and a musket. A full uniform and the rudiments of drill were acquired after the battle, though *Hardee's Tactics* remained unmastered until the recruit committed the boner of not presenting arms to General Beauregard while on outpost duty, and thus revealed his deficiency to an embarrassed captain.

In the process of becoming soldiers Wood and his comrades informally organized themselves into small groups known as messes. These were composed of about eight men drawn together by ties of congeniality. They ate together, played together, fought together and were welded by common hardships into tight little families that looked unfailingly to their mutual welfare. The members usually acquired nicknames. In Wood's mess William Perley, owing to a pronounced inclination of appetite revealed early in the war, was dubbed "Frog Legs" and Joe Birchhead was known as "Beaury" after General Beauregard. Sergeant Alexander Hoffman—not in the mess, but a good friend of Wood—was called "Pig." If Wood himself acquired a nickname, he does not divulge it. A passage in the reminiscences suggests that his comrades called him "Big I," but the manuscript version does not contain this sobriquet—which seems rather to have originated with Wood after the war.

A remarkable thing about Wood's original mess of eight members is that all but one survived the war (Thomas G. Wertenbaker died of illness in 1862) and were still living in 1895.

Early in 1862, in anticipation of the end of its original term of service, the Nineteenth Virginia was reorganized and inducted "for three years or the war." As a part of the reorganization the men elected their officers. In token of their respect and esteem, Wood's comrades in Company "A" elevated him to the position of junior second lieutenant, or "third lieutenant" as the rank was sometimes designated. Shortly afterward he was designated acting regimental adjutant, which position he held until the summer of 1862 when he returned to Company "A." He retained his place in "Mess No. 1," even while serving as adjutant.

The manuscript of Wood's reminiscences, only a part of which has been preserved, relates an amusing incident of the war's first winter that does not appear in the printed version. As the manuscript recounts it, the regimental band leader—a man named Teltow—on one occasion imbibed too freely of apple-jack. Under the influence of this potent delicacy, Teltow became obsessed with the conviction that band leaders were underpaid and their importance not sufficiently recognized by the army. He finally decided that the matter was of such moment that he should register a personal protest with Colonel J. B. Strange, the regimental commander. His comrades tried to dissuade him, but to no avail. "He staggered to the Col's. quarters and pulled aside the tent flap that was serving for a door and poking his head in exclaimed—'Strange, you are a damned old louse.' " When the bandmaster sobered up he found himself in the guard house.

In the spring of 1862 the Nineteenth Virginia left winter quarters and headed for Williamsburg to help repel McClellan. As Colonel Strange led his men on the march he passed General J. E. B. Stuart, a fact which drew from that rollicking cavalryman the quip: "It is Strange—passing strange." This incident, according to Wood, "provoked a laugh near akin to a yell."

At Williamsburg the regiment experienced its first real fighting. Now a part of General George E. Pickett's brigade —made up of the Eighth, Eighteenth, Nineteenth, Twenty-eighth and Fifty-sixth Virginia Regiments—the Nineteenth acquitted itself well by capturing a battery. Lieutenant Wood was in the thick of this action, dashing about with orders of his superiors. Just after the battery was taken Sergeant "Pig" Hoffman was shot down, the first member of Company "A" to be killed in battle.

Seven Pines was the regiment's next battle, and here too the fighting was hot. Company "A" lost four killed and its total casualties amounted to twenty per cent of its effective strength. "On no future occasion," according to Wood, "was our loss so great in so short a time."

Less than a month later came the series of engagements about Richmond known as the Seven Days. At the beginning of this period, Wood had his first contact with General Robert E. Lee. Unfortunately he did not then recognize the "courtly gentleman" who politely requested him to carry a message. At Gaines' Mill Wood was often exposed to great danger as he discharged his adjutant's duties. In this fight Company "A" was guilty of lagging when an advance was ordered but the defection was momentary and, according to Wood, this was the one and only time that his company ever hesitated in a charge. Fortunately for Wood and his comrades the Nineteenth filled only a secondary role at Malvern Hill where Lee made "his great tactical mistake."

But the Seven Days saved Richmond and gave the men of Lee's army increased confidence in themselves and their leaders. "Why did McClellan not take Richmond?" they asked, then exultingly quoted the Richmond *Examiner* in reply: "Because there was a Pickett to pass, two Hills to cross, rough Rodes to overcome, a Longstreet to travel and a Strange by path across the Gulley (ordnance officer of the Nineteenth Virginia)."

After Malvern Hill the Nineteenth enjoyed only a brief respite before engaging in another tremendous battle at Manassas. At Second Manassas Wood commanded Company "A," though he mentions the fact only incidentally. His performance must have been creditable as he was temporarily placed over two companies in the subsequent march toward Maryland. On this march he became involved in an altercation with the regimental commander. Strict orders had been issued against straggling but on a night march one of Wood's men wandered ahead of his comrades and when the fact was reported to Colonel Strange that officer curtly ordered the lieutenant to consider himself under arrest. The next morning the colonel sent his compliments and directed Wood to return to duty. Instead the lieutenant sent back the reply: "Present my compliments to the Colonel and inform him that I question his right to put me under arrest for the offense mentioned, and therefore decline to resume my duties and demand a court of inquiry"—which, even granting that the arrest may have been ill-advised, was a remarkable statement for a "junior second lieutenant" to address to a full colonel. But the Civil War was full of incidents that today seem fantastic. In the ensuing fight at Boonsboro, on September 14, Strange was killed, and Wood immediately afterward was restored to duty. In the meantime, he had ignored his arrest to the extent of participating in the Boonsboro fight "on something of an independent style."

Despite Lee's stringent orders to the contrary, straggling was notoriously prevalent on the Maryland campaign. The Nineteenth Virginia was reduced to about fifty men when it entered the bloody Sharpsburg fight on September 17. Wood states that he was in command of the regiment at Sharpsburg and his statement is substantiated by the official report of General R. B. Garnett who had succeeded to the command of Pickett's brigade. But the report of the regiment's participation in the battle submitted by Captain B. Brown was indorsed to General Garnett by Acting Regimental Adjutant James D. McIntire with the statement: "The regiment was acting more directly under your orders than those of its commander Captain Brown, who was present during the engagement. I did not recognize Adjutant Wood as its commander on that day, he being only third lieutenant."

Wood unquestionably commanded the regiment at Sharpsburg, but McIntire's indorsement suggests that his incurring that responsibility was due to the defection of others of higher rank. Wood says nothing directly on the point in his reminiscences, but a letter to his homefolk of November 4, 1862, indicates that all was not as it should be with respect to fellow officers in the company. "I am still the same old Nat," he stated, "and with the help of God I will stand by my boys until the last gun is fired. . . . I have been shamefully forsaken by my Company officers, but still I have in the Company men who will stand by me as long as life last. . . . if it were not flattering myself I would say that I am respected by my fellow officers as highly as anyone in the Regiment."

The letter of November 4 also gives a glimpse of the hardship experienced by Wood on the Maryland campaign. After requesting that clothing, soap and other articles be sent to him, he stated: "I have not changed Socks for two months and I am compelled to borrow Shirts & Drawers to get mine washed. I have lost so much clothing that I sometimes think of being a negro at once and be done with it . . . . I have marched, fought, Slept and eat like someone destitute of all traits of Civilization but it was because great demands were made upon us and we had to stand up to the Rack or be whipped by the cowardly Yankees." Despite his destitute condition, his morale was still high. "I am an advocate of Peace," he declared, "but before I will Submit to the rule of Abraham Lincoln I will spend my life in Camp with all its hardships & privations." As insurance against excessive discomfort, however, he asked his homefolk in this letter to be on the lookout for a Negro body servant whom he proposed to hire for fifteen dollars a month. He had previously had the services of a colored aide for a time but apparently was not able to get a replacement.

In his reminiscences, Wood jumps from the close of the Sharpsburg fight to the preliminaries of the Gettysburg campaign. During this period the Army of Northern Virginia fought the battles of Fredericksburg and Chancellorsville, but the Nineteenth Virginia was relatively inactive from October, 1862, to June, 1863. Pickett's Division, of which the regiment was a part, was in reserve at Fredericksburg and a few weeks later it went with other parts of Longstreet's Corps on a foraging expedition to Southwestern Virginia and Eastern North Carolina. This expedition was not completed until after Chancellorsville.

Pickett's Division did not reach Gettysburg in time for the first two days fighting, but played a conspicuous role in the gallant climax of July 3. The colonel of the Nineteenth Virginia, Henry Gantt, was incapacitated by a wound early in the action and Lieutenant Colonel John T. Ellis who succeeded to command was killed in the artillery duel that preceded the assault. The brigade commander, the heroic Garnett, fell at the peak of the charge. But as previously noted, Wood was so absorbed in his own determined effort to get at the enemy's lines that he was hardly aware of these and the countless other casualties that littered the approach to Cemetery Ridge on that fateful day. And after the charge was repulsed he was equally absorbed in a desperate effort to get back to the protection of the Confederate position. He was lucky to return alive, with only a bruise and a scratch, for his already depleted regiment suffered a loss of ten killed and thirty-four wounded. Company "A," according to Wood, "was small indeed, the next morning as an effort was made to get the men together," and "Major Peyton was senior officer of the regiment—fit for duty —if not of the brigade."

After the return from Gettysburg, Wood and his comrades enjoyed a well earned period of tranquility and rest. In September, 1863, they went into camp at Chaffin's Farm near Richmond where they remained, except for brief interludes, when called on to help repel Federal raids, until late May, 1864. Established in comfortable log cabins inherited from Wise's Brigade, their predecessors at the Chaffin's Farm camp site, members of the Nineteenth Virginia "lived at home." The more domestically inclined kept cows and chickens and dabbled at gardening while those of festive bent indulged in parties, visiting, musical sessions, card playing, sports and games. Furloughs to Richmond, supplemented by unauthorized trips made by what was known in camp parlance as "running the blockade," afforded further relief from camp routine. During the winter rations were sometimes short, a circumstance which prompted some members of the Nineteenth to try to convert into "boiled venison" a fat cat that frequented their camp. For two days the kettle was kept boiling, but the old cat seemed only to grow tougher "and the dinner was spoiled."

The first battle of 1864 in which the Nineteenth Virginia participated was Second Cold Harbor on June 3. Wood took over command of Company "A" when Captain Gulick was wounded early in the fight, and in the latter part of the action he was called on temporarily to command Company "K" as that organization had lost all its officers. Apparently some of the higher officers of the regiment shirked their duty in this battle, as the command of the regiment devolved on the senior captain, J. G. Woodson, who was killed during the fight. When shortly afterward a report, sent in seemingly by one of the absent officers, was published in a Richmond paper, it failed to mention Woodson's being in command. Wood and some of his associates were infuriated by what they construed as a slight to a gallant captain who though ill on the day of battle had unhesitatingly assumed a responsibility that had cost him his life. So, a protest, stating simply that Woodson had been in command of the Nineteenth Virginia when he was slain, was published over the signature of Wood and two captains. The colonel of the regiment was displeased by this act and when Wood revealed that he was the author of the piece, the colonel vented his displeasure on the lieutenant— but by what means Wood does not reveal.

After a brief period of maneuvering about Petersburg, fighting became static and Wood and his comrades settled down to a long stint of trench warfare. To ease the tedium of this new but unglamorous existence, the soldiers developed a lively trade with their opposites in blue, the principle items of exchange being Southern for Northern newspapers and tobacco for coffee. Wood and his intimates found diversion in Masonic meetings, religious services, debating, reading, athletic contests, checkers and chess. One of the relics brought home from the war by Wood was a set of chessmen made in camp during this last winter of the war. In his reminiscences he states that "several men learned to play a good game of chess while blindfolded."

In late March, 1865, Wood's brigade, now commanded by General Eppa Hunton, was ordered from the trenches to meet a new and pressing threat of the Federals. In the fighting that ensued, Wood received a wound in the neck which proved to be slight, but which gave him his only permanent war scar. Hunton's brigade was not in the battle of Five Forks and, as Wood put it, "consequently did not share *the defeat of the war* by Pickett's division." In the disorganization that followed the Federal break-through, the remnant of the brigade was surrounded and captured at Sailor's Creek, April 6, 1865.

Wood was imprisoned first in Washington and then at Johnson's Island. He was released June 20, 1865, on taking the oath of allegiance, and returned to his home where he "was glad to don some clean citizen's clothes . . . and to eat a good dinner."

For the first few years of peace, Wood worked in Charlottesville, presumably for his pre-war employer, John C. Patterson. He then went to New York City where he was a clerk in a jewelry firm for a short time, after which he found employment in Baltimore as a salesman for the James Carey Company.

In the meantime, on August 9, 1870, Wood married Nannie Bullock, an attractive woman of 21 (he was 30) from Louisa County, Virginia, with whom he had been carrying on a lively correspondence for several years. Because of the long separations from his wife which his Baltimore job entailed, Wood moved to Charlottesville in the early 1870's and took a position as clerk in the University Book Store. A few years later he became a farmer in Louisa County and followed that occupation until about 1883, when he took over the operation of Poindexter's store in the northern part of the county. About 1891 he returned to Charlottesville where he went into business for a time with his brother Lewellen. He afterward became a bookkeeper, first for the Charlottesville *Chronicle* and then for the R. F. Harris Foundry. He worked for the Harris firm until he was incapacitated by illness shortly before his death. He died in Charlottesville on February 10, 1909, when seventy years of age, and after funeral services in the First Baptist Church he was laid to rest by fellow members of Masonic Lodge Number 60. He was survived by his wife, who lived until February 7, 1938, and two daughters, Mrs. W. U. Parkinson and Miss Emma Garnett Wood. The last, named for Wood's beloved commander, R. B. Garnett, still lives in the old family residence in Charlottesville.

Wood's own writings, the official record of his war service, the recollections of his daughter and other scattered evidence, afford a substantial basis for evaluating the man and the soldier. In his army days Wood was not large—he weighed only 127 pounds when he entered the service—but he was of handsome appearance, with expressive blue eyes and a well-shaped head, topped by an abundant growth of light hair, which was matched by a fine set of whiskers. As he grew older his weight increased and he lost much of his hair. But his eyes retained their youthful expressiveness.

Always he had a rich sense of humor, though this is not as apparent in his reminiscences as in his letters and conversation. In a letter to a brother written early in the war he stated: "Were I at home I might be your Rival. Make hay while the Sun Shines. *Court* Mollie."

From his boyhood he was deeply religious. The mess to which he belonged throughout the war was known as "the Camp Meeting Mess" because of its practice of holding "regular family worship" each night before retiring. After the war he was an active member of the Baptist church, and for a number of years served as deacon of the First Baptist Church of Charlottesville. His habits were good, though he does not seem to have been a prude. In his memoirs he tells with obvious pleasure of excessive indulgence in cherry bounce while on the Maryland Campaign but he leaves the impression that this was a unique experience for him, and apparently it was. His religious and moral views were not such as to restrict him to a dull and narrow existence. Throughout his active life he fished, hunted, played chess and participated fully in Masonic meetings and similar activities of his friends and neighbors. His home life was exceedingly congenial, and one of his most enjoyable diversions was a quiet evening of whist or checkers with his wife and daughters.

As a soldier he was dependable, loyal and courageous. His obituary in the Charlottesville *Daily Progress* of February 10, 1909, states: "It is probable that no braver soldier ever lived," and when later the same year Charles C. Wertenbaker, a close associate throughout the war, wrote a preface for *Reminiscences of Big I,* he asserted that Wood never missed a battle in which his company engaged, and "seemed to be without fear, even in positions of the most appalling danger."

The question naturally presents itself: why did a man of such gallantry and ability not rise to higher rank than first lieutenant? The question seems especially pertinent when it is recalled that Wood led his company in several major battles and at Sharpsburg commanded his regiment. The explanation lies apparently in two principal considerations. First, Captain John C. Culin, though wounded in battle after battle, retained command of Company "A" until the end of the war and thus prevented Wood's elevation to captain by the usual route of promotion. Of course the regimental commander might have put Wood in line for promotion by transferring him to another company. The fact of this not having been done suggests the second probable reason for Wood's failure to rise above lieutenant: This was a certain outspokenness which brought him into disfavor with some of his strategically placed superiors. His demand for a court of inquiry in September, 1862, offended Colonel Strange and though this commander shortly became a casualty, the incident was known to his successors and may have influenced their relations with Wood. Then, in 1864, Wood incurred the wrath of another colonel, and possibly other members of the regimental staff, by publishing a protest against the treatment of Captain J. G. Woodson. Wood also may have been hindered by lack of support from some of his fellow officers in the company. Certainly this possibility is suggested by the lieutenant's letter to his homefolk of November 4, 1862. Be that as it may, Wood seems to have had the solid respect both during the war and afterward of most of the officers and men who served in close association with him. Among the personal papers of Wood preserved by his descendants is a petition of his comrades for his promotion to first lieutenant.

The title of Wood's reminiscences might create the impression that he was boastful, but the narrative itself reveals no tendency toward vanity or egotism. He apparently adopted the title because of its catchiness and uniqueness.

These memoirs are not as rich or as vivid as are some of the other personal narratives that came out of the Civil War. Indeed, they are not as good as Wood might have made them had he let his flair for story telling have the full play that is revealed in his letters and unpublished fragments of his reminiscences. He was evidently restrained by the fact that he was writing for publication. He omitted from the published version an account of the regimental band leader getting drunk and calling the colonel a damned old louse. He also left out a reference to a raid that he and some comrades made on a Virginia cornfield and peach orchard early in the war and a chance meeting of himself and Sergeant Hoffman with John S. Mosby after which Hoffman spoke of Mosby as a "trifling fellow" and "that poor wretch Jack Mosby." Other items appearing in the manuscript and not included in the book are: the bringing into camp of a piece of shoat by Comrade Dagon with the explanation, "I let no pig bite me;" the statement that Colonel George Watson Carr was a "red tape" officer and an account of how the regiment found a means of embarrassing this officer at dress parade; and the story of a drinking spree some members of Company "A" enjoyed. It is to be surmised that these items were deleted to prevent injury or offense to the persons involved or their descendants. And it is possible that the editing was done by someone other than Wood.

But the fact that the account was written for publication while persons familiar with the events were still living also had its benefits. The knowledge that every statement might be checked by comrades surely must have encouraged Wood's normal inclination to accuracy.

Notwithstanding a slightly roseate quality, Wood's narrative is in general an honest, and straightforward representation of Confederate experience from the viewpoint of an intelligent company officer.

———

Reminiscences of Big I apparently was written in the 1890's, though portions of the manuscript may have been drafted earlier. The account was prepared originally for publication in the Charlottesville *Progress* which ran it serially over a period from April to December, 1895. In 1909, shortly after Wood's death, the narrative was printed in a book of 107 pages by the Michie Company of Charlottesville. The book was privately printed in an edition of 200 copies. These were circulated among friends and relatives of Wood, and were not offered for sale. For a long time the work has been virtually unobtainable. The copy here reproduced was obtained on interlibrary loan from the University of Virginia.

In preparing Wood's narrative for reissue I have followed closely the text of the first edition. The few changes that were made consisted largely of correcting what appears to have been printer's errors or slips of the author's pen, such as Cab Run (Cub Run), Tailor's Creek (Sailor's Creek), Chafin's Farm (Chaffin's Farm) and Colonel Henry Garnett (Colonel Henry Gantt).

For assistance in the preparation of the new edition I am deeply indebted to Miss Emma G. Wood of Charlottesville. Miss Wood generously supplied essential biographical data along with letters, pictures and other personal documents of her parents. She also made available all of the original manuscript of the reminiscences that is extant, which includes the material making up the first twenty pages of the printed version (first edition) with scattered portions of the remainder—in all something less than half of the total narrative.

I am indebted to the Adjutant General, Department of the Army, for information about Wood's war service. Information provided by Miss Wood and the Adjutant General was supplemented by material gleaned from *The War of the Rebellion: A Compilation of the Official Records of the Union and Confederate Armies,* unit histories and personal narratives. John Cook Wyllie, Curator of Rare Books, the Alderman Library, University of Virginia, gave valuable help and encouragement throughout the editing process. I am especially indebted to him for putting me in touch with William H. Runge, an assistant in the Alderman Library and now a graduate student in history at the University of Virginia. Mr. Runge interviewed Miss Wood for me, located an obituary of William N. Wood in the Charlottesville *Daily Progress,* secured illustrative material and laboriously dug out precious nuggets of information from obscure sources. Without his efficient and unstinted help *Reminiscences of Big I* could not have been reissued in the form here presented.

Emory University   Bell Irvin Wiley
5 January 1955

REMINISCENCES OF BIG I

PREFACE

Learning that the following articles, written by my comrade, W. N. Wood, are to be put in book form, I am anxious to give its readers a sketch of his character and of his merits as a soldier, so that the young men of the future may know of what material the famous army of Northern Virginia, commanded by the immortal Robert E. Lee, was composed.

William Nathaniel Wood was born in the northern part of Albemarle County, Va., November 16th, 1839, and died on February 10th, 1909. He entered mercantile life when quite young, in the town of Charlottesville, where one of his first employers, Mr. John C. Patterson, still resides.

Wood entered the Monticello Guard of Charlottesville, Co. A, Nineteenth Virginia Regiment, on July 20th, 1861, the evening before the first battle of Manassas, and had his "baptism of fire" the next day. All through the war, he was attentive to his duty, and seemed to be without fear, even in positions of the most appalling danger.

He was soon promoted to a Lieutenancy, and for much of the latter part of the war, was in command of the Company. At the battle of Gettysburg, after Captain Culin was wounded, he commanded the company, and led it to the stone wall, and what is more wonderful, he went back under the most terrific fire from the stone wall and on each flank. His clothing was riddled with shot, but he escaped with a slight scratch under one arm.

Wood was, I think, in every encounter in which his company was engaged during the whole war, and he, with what was left of it, was captured at Sailor's Creek, April 6th, 1865, just three days before Lee's surrender.

It was the custom of Wood's mess to have family prayers every night. All of the members of the mess were humble, earnest Christians. In a word, Lieutenant Wood was a good citizen, a good Christian, and, as a soldier, was a hero, a good Mason, and an honest man. This was the universal estimate of his character, by his fellow-citizens, as it certainly is of his comrade and friend,

C. C. Wertenbaker

Charlottesville, Va.,
    June 17th, 1909.

Big I To The Front

On Thursday, July 18th, I left Charlottesville to join the army. Arrived at Manassas junction on the evening of the same day, and was greeted by the booming of artillery at or near Union Mills on the Bull Run, a few miles distant. This small engagement, though some distance off, was enough to give rise to the feeling "I would like to be at home." Spent the night at Manassas, and next morning joined the Monticello Guard—Company A, Nineteenth Virginia Regiment—at Lewis' ford on Bull Run. Spent most of the day visiting the boys. On the 20th I was ordered by Captain W. B. Mallory to take my turn in throwing up breastworks. Putting on a pair of buck gloves I worked most earnestly for a few minutes, but the July sun was so intense that I welcomed the "relief" most cordially. All my life I had been small for my age—sparely built and not strong, and weighed at this time 127 pounds, though twenty-one years old. My white shirt, standing collar and hair parted behind gave the boys a target for good-

1

humored jests which were as good-humoredly received. That night I slept soundly with Comrade W. C. Payne, with the starry decked heavens as a canopy, as an initiation into camp life.

Sunday morning, July 21st, I was awakened by the unearthly sound of a piece of artillery which was supposed to be at the inconvenient distance of a mile or so. Without paying much attention to my toilet, I took my place in the trenches with a minnie musket in my hand. I had never drilled an hour, and the mysteries of keeping the step and loading in nine times were things unknown to me. There I was, however, a soldier only in position—in all else, possibly, the greenest of the awkward squad. I wore a brown frock coat, and a pair of black cassimere pants, and save a miserably sunburning cap, wore nothing of a soldier's garb. These things flashed through my mind and I remember wishing the enemy would not try to cross at this ford. Some meat and bread were brought us, of which I ate heartily, not failing to compare my breakfast with that usually furnished by mine host Smith of the Central Hotel.

My next recollection is an order from the Captain, "Don't put your head above the works," which I conscientiously obeyed. Joe Slayton created quite a sensation by exclaiming, "Yonder they come, Captain, let me shoot, let me shoot!" One "Yank" had appeared at the edge of the pines on the other side of a small field that lay immediately in our front on the opposite side of Bull Run. The pines were said to be full of them, but in obedience to the Captain's orders, I made no extensive examination, and cannot vouch for the report. Again Joe Slayton saw them coming, and wanted to shoot. Then was heard the roar of the enemy's "Long Tom," and a cannon ball whistled over our heads and buried itself in the hill-side in our rear. One piece of Latham's battery, situated immediately to the left of Company A, now opened in earnest, and such a noise it made! whilst away up the Run (to our left) the mus-

LIEUT. WILLIAM N. WOOD,
Company A, Nineteenth Virginia Infantry
—*Courtesy Miss Emma G. Wood, Charlottesville, Va.*

GENERAL ROBERT E. LEE ON TRAVELLER

"The courtly gentleman whom I met under the apple tree," at Gaines' Mill, June 27, 1862, "without recognizing."

—Photograph by Miley. Courtesy Virginia Historical Society

GENERAL RICHARD B. GARNETT

At Gettysburg, "Our brigade commander, General R. B. Garnett, was killed near the enemy's line. . . . a noble specimen of manhood. His memory is perpetuated in my household by my youngest child bearing his name."

—From Photographic History of the Civil War

GENERAL GEORGE E. PICKETT

After the fateful charge at Gettysburg, "when General Pickett silently extended his hand, and . . . almost sobbed out the words, 'My brave men! My brave men!,' I felt that after all we were not disgraced."

GENERAL EPPA HUNTON

Thirty-seven years after the war, on a visit to the Bull Run battlefield, "Had a long talk with General Eppa Hunton (my old brigade commander) in which battles were fought again."

—Courtesy National Archives

GENERAL P. G. T. BEAUREGARD
"Was that General Beauregard? And what is making a salute anyway?"

PICKETT'S CH

"The enemy's line . . . is just in front .

GETTYSBURG
n I received a blow on the right leg."
—*Courtesy National Archives*

GENERAL J. E. B. STUART

Enroute to Williamsburg, May 3, 1862, "With Colonel Strange riding at the head of the regiment, we passed General J. E. B. Stuart who remarked: 'It is strange—passing strange,' which provoked a laugh near akin to a yell."

—*Courtesy National Archives*

THE CONRAD HOUSE, BATTLEFIELD OF FIRST MANASSAS

"In rear of this house . . . nine companies of the Nineteenth Virginia Regiment formed a line of battle near the close of the fight."

—*Courtesy John R. Peacock, High Point, N. C.*

RUINS OF THE HENRY HOUSE, BATTLEFIELD OF FIRST BULL RUN.

Here, thirty-seven years after the battle, "I stood for a while . . . . and mused; within a stone's throw was the heaviest fighting."

—*Photograph by Brady. Courtesy National Archives*

OLD CAPITOL PRISON, WASHINGTON, D. C.

"My few days there were not comfortable. . . . We were fed on pork and beans and hard tack."

—*Photograph by Brady. Courtesy National Archives*

JOHNSON'S ISLAND PRISON

"As the war was over, discipline was relaxed, and 'we boys' had very good times." From Henry Howe, *Historical Collections of Ohio.*

—*Courtesy Chicago Historical Society*

Set of chessmen made in camp in the winter of 1864-1865 and used by Wood and his comrades.

Photo by Ralph R. Thompson, University, Virginia
—Courtesy Miss Emma Wood, Charlottesville, Va.

WILLIAM N. WOOD AND HIS WIFE, NANNIE BULLOCK WOOD

—Courtesy Miss Emma G. Wood, Charlottesville, Va.

ketry had made a feeble effort to add to the din and confusion. The July sun was giving us full benefit of its rays.

The sound of artillery was more and more frequent. The musketry, away to the left, was increasing, and Gray Latham was sending shot and shell to the pines in our front. Things were getting warm, and Captain Latham exclaimed, "Barton, the battle of Waterloo was nothing! Ten pins is nowhere! Don't let 'Lazy Joe' talk so much," referring to one of his pieces further to the left.

Just here, in the midst of the increased sound of musketry on the left of the line, the "talking" of "Lazy Joe" near us, and the belching of "Long Tom" in our front, Company A was ordered out of the trenches and formed a line of battle on the side of the hill just in rear of our former position. For what purpose I have never learned. In a few minutes, however, we were returned to the trenches which was done with alacrity. Just about this time our Colonel John B. Strange called out to his Sergeant-Major, Joe Lipop, "Lipop! I am without orders, what shall I do?" Lipop replied, "Retreat to Manassas as quickly as possible." This advice was not taken, however, and orders soon came which called us from the trenches and toward the musketry which had become much heavier and nearer. Striking a small branch we marched up its left bank and out of sight of the enemy, as we thought, but we had not proceeded far when a stray bullet from the direction of the enemy killed—, of an Amherst company, who was the first dead man I saw on the field of battle. About this time one of those stray bullets struck Jack Collier of Company A on the head, making a small flesh wound. Volunteers to look after our wounded comrade were plentiful, one man declaring he had the very medicine for him. The "very medicine" proved to be a bottle of "No. 6."

Thirsty, hot, still somewhat frightened, we continued our march up the branch for some distance, then filed to the right through a small body of woods into a field in front of the Chinn house and formed a line of battle. The Newton battery came dashing up, and unlimbered in our front and began a rapid fire upon the foe. The firing ceased, the smoke vanished and then the prettiest sight I ever witnessed was before us. The enemy in full flight, running with might and main and rapidly increasing the distance between us. As they ran a few shots from the battery last mentioned added much to their confusion, and hurried them up the hill, homeward bound. Our regiment marched in pursuit and made a detour north of the pike, but did not come up with the flying foe.

On this march we passed piles of knapsacks, blankets, &c., where the enemy had left them in the morning.

I had not fired a gun, but always claimed I was in the first battle of Manassas.

CHAPTER II

Camp Life

Monday, July 22, 1861, was a very rainy day. Battles were usually followed by rain, but this, our first engagement of any magnitude, was followed by the heaviest rain of any battle during the war.

I got permission to spend two hours on the battle-field, and for the first time saw the dreadful effects of terrible war. Just east of the Henry house the dead were most numerous. I wandered over the hotly-contested grounds, and when informed by a knowing comrade that this great victory would secure our independence I rejoiced in the thought that no more scenes of death and destruction were to offend my vision, and no more such suffering as the hospital display would curdle my blood, "Where ignorance is bliss," etc.

I returned to our camp at Lewis' ford with a good overcoat, a splendid canteen and a good oil cloth, all of which were destined to do service under much more trying circumstances, and to be used in ordeals more severe.

5

We remained at Lewis' ford the 23d and 24th, and on the 25th moved to Cub Run. Here I learned the manual of arms and, in fact, mastered the company drill of Hardee's tactics. Not far from our camp on Cub Run was a pond of water and hither resorted the lovers of frog legs. Here it was that William Perley became so well known as "Frog Leg Perley." R. C. Vandegrift was probably loudest in his denunciation of feeding on frog legs, until one luckless hour he was induced to taste and try, when lo! what a change. Perley's ingenuity was taxed to the utmost in making excuses for not accommodating a friend with the craved morsel.

While encamped on Cub Run I was detailed one morning for guard duty, and was posted on a "beat" near an old Virginia residence of pretentious appearances. No instructions were given me. I had nothing to do but to walk the "beat" from the locust tree to the corner of the garden and to bear myself with all the dignity of a soldier. A path from the residence to a spring in the bottom below crossed my beat. The walking became monotonous and my musket became heavy. In the midst of an attempt to improve on Hardee in handling arms a middle-aged gentleman of medium size, of dark or brown complexion, with piercing or cutting black eyes passed down the path. I noticed his intent observation of my presence, but soon ceased to think of him. In a short time he passed back from the spring and entered the house. Though near the path I said nothing and did nothing. Scarcely had the stranger entered the house when Lieutenant John Culin, the officer of the guard, came at full speed from guard quarters, and exclaimed: "Sentinel! do you know what you have done?" I replied, "I have done nothing for nearly two hours but kill grass along this beat." "Why, you have allowed General Beauregard to pass you without making a salute." "Was that General Beauregard? and what is making a salute anyway?" There and then that efficient officer and superb drill-master instructed me in the art of saluting superiors. This was the first time I saw General Beauregard.

A few days after this I was detailed for out-post duty, and now recall the sensation of having no one between myself and the enemy. I was sent to camp that evening for the countersign for the night, which was furnished me by the Regimental Adjutant—the accomplished soldier and gentleman—Charley Wertenbaker. I doubtless felt my importance as I returned to the out-post with the three-cornered paper in which was folded the word "Madrid" which had been given me orally also. The Sergeant only awaited my return to post the first relief for the night. The countersign was given each sentinel as he was located at his post. Two hours rolled around and my time for duty came. I relieved William F. Gordon of Company B, and was much alarmed when he said: "Big I, are you certain the word was given you Mad-rid? for the correct pronunciation is Ma-drid." Thus I was on out-post for the first time at night, and with all the imagined evils of uncertainty as to the correct pronunciation of the capital of Spain. My two hours passed, however, as did my next two during the night without the occasion of testing the correctness of the word.

An alarm one night caused the company to be called out. "Fall in! fall in!" sang out Henry Dade, and such packing up and hurrying to and fro! for the report had come that the enemy was advancing. Tip Collier came running to the Captain with a well-packed champagne basket on his shoulder and some cooking utensils under his arm. "Captain! what shall I do with my gun for I have more than I can carry? It was a false alarm, and at the next dress parade there was read an order to send extra baggage to Manassas.

Joe Birckhead—known in the regiment as Beaury—was on camp guard one night when the Colonel conceived the idea of testing the efficiency of the sentinels. Passing out of camp he attempted to return across Beaury's beat. In stentorian tones—"Halt!—who comes there?" rang out from the sentry. "Colonel Strange without the countersign," was the reply, "Mark time, Colonel Strange, mark time! Corporal of the guard—post No. 4." And the Colonel had to mark time until the corporal of the guard came to his relief.

Cub Run camp proved unhealthy, and we moved forward late in August and went into camp north of Fairfax Courthouse, where we suffered severely with measles and fever. Company A lost Mat Sales, Joe Fuller and McMullen by death, and many sick were sent to the rear.

Camp-duty became more irksome, false alarms more frequent, and the picket duty on Mason's and Munson's hills gave exercise in abundance. Who does not remember the "Up the hill and down again and no blood spilt" of Colonel Strange? or the "Attention, my people, fall in, them fellows are a-coming;" or the more original command of Colonel Preston of the Twenty-Eighth, "Fall in Twenty-Eighth, fall in!" and raising his voice as he exclaimed, "If you don't fall in I will march the regiment off and leave every one of you behind!"

My next will include the battle of Williamsburg.

CHAPTER III

Winter Quarters—The Battle Of Williamsburg

The fall season had come. The Twelfth Virginia Regiment did much picket duty at Mason's and Munson's hills. One moonless night I was detailed for out-post duty north of Munson's hill. My post was on a path leading down a hill which was covered with ivy—a regular ivy thicket. At the bottom of the hill was a stream of water large enough to turn a mill. Beyond this stream the imagination peopled the country with "our friends, the enemy." I was instructed to listen and observe. It was chilly and no fire allowed. It was lonesome. Orders positive not to move from that stump. The nearest sentinel a hundred yards away. Not a star to enliven the scene. The hours passed slowly. I distinctly heard a noise, as if some one was opening the ivy bushes not far to my right —then a twig broke not far from me. Pit-a-pat went my heart—great, cold waves passed up the spinal cord. Noiselessly

9

I cocked my minnie, eagerly I bent forward to catch another sound, which came again as a fox (I suppose) trotted off to the rear.

We went into winter quarters near Centreville and the companies divided into messes; each mess being allowed to build a hut. Our mess consisted of R. C. Vandegrift, Thomas G. Wertenbaker, James Perley, Joseph F. Birckhead, George Thomas Johnson, James Brown, W. T. Jones and W. N. Wood. With one single exception they are all living at this time (1895). Many of them were badly wounded, but only one of them disqualified for active service by wounds. The exception mentioned above was Thomas Grady Wertenbaker, the brightest and best of the lot, who died of disease in 1862 (see Johnson's University Memorial). This was mess No. 1 of Company A, but was dubbed "The Camp Meeting Mess," because they had regular family worship before retiring at night.

Of the many ludicrous incidents that I have written out, the following is selected as one of the best: John Hill, William Cloa, Buck Bailey, William Vaughan and John Dodd had been put in the guard house for some trivial offense. Captain Mallory got permission from the Colonel to have them get wood for the Captain's mess. The boys went at it with a will and a good pile of wood appeared at the Captain's door, but upon investigation every stick was found to be black-gum and therefore almost worthless. A good joke on the Captain. The joke was turned on the boys, however, when they were ordered to return to the Captain's shanty and split every stick—for splitting black-gum is one of the things not easy to do. The matter was compromised, however, by the boys going to the pines and getting good wood.

"The Camp Meeting Mess" had a few books, a set of chess men, took one daily paper and kept on hand a supply of writing materials. They became experts in making loaf bread and telling yarns—this last accomplishment survives.

The winter passed, and in February I received my re-enlisted furlough and made my first visit home. Rejoined my command in Orange county in March (1862). Very soon we started for the peninsula. Though late in March it snowed and rained, the mud was deep, the streams were swollen and the bridges washed away. In such a wretched condition were the roads, that our commissary wagons under charge of Maj. R. H. Jones could not get to us the night we encamped near Louisa Courthouse. We secured some flour, however, by "hook or crook," and proceeded to "make it up" on an oil cloth, and baked the bread on flat rocks set up before the fire. I tried the experiment (successfully) of winding the dough around a nicely scraped dog-wood stick and turning it around in front of the fire until it was baked.

We marched to Richmond where we took boats for the peninsula, arriving on Magruder's line about the 12th of April. Here Company A was organized. John C. Culin was elected Captain—defeating C. C. Wertenbaker on the seventh ballot—by one vote. Big I was elected junior second lieutenant, and was assigned to duty as regimental adjutant, but retaining membership in the mess. We did picket duty and waded in mud and slush until the welcomed orders came which started us toward Richmond on May the third. With Colonel Strange riding at the head of the regiment we passed General J. E. B. Stuart, who remarked: "It is Strange—passing strange," which provoked a laugh near akin to a yell.

On the fourth of May we arrived in the immediate vicinity of Williamsburg where we spent the night. What a still night this was. No firing on picket line. No Yorktown artillery to disturb our slumbers as William Jones and myself drew our blankets over us. We afterwards learned the significance of quiet, for it frequently preceded fighting.

The fifth of May opened with rain and discomfort. About ten o'clock the regiment was formed and marched into Williamsburg and rested "in place" for awhile. Suddenly there broke upon the ear the sound of musketry and artillery. Couriers passed at a gallop, officers became active, and everything indicated seriousness. "Attention! forward, march!" and we headed toward the noise of battle. The firing increased as we approached. Leaving Fort Magruder on our left we passed across an open field which was under the enemy's artillery. Shells were bursting and solid shot was ploughing mother earth just where we had to go. In front and to the left clouds of dust gave some indication of the danger into which at a double-quick we were rushing. We passed the exposed point, however, without the loss of a man and were quickly shielded by the friendly forest. We halted and formed a line of battle in the field with the woods immediately in front. Marching forward in line for the first time as Pickett's brigade, we felt strong and hoped our very appearance would cause the enemy to fly. These fellows were not made that way, however, but doggedly held their position and awaited our approach. Over the fence we went and through the woods with a steady step until we came to where the trees had been felled for an opening in front of Fort Magruder. Then we stopped. Just in front, in a road running through the felled timbers was a beautiful line of battle awaiting us. The Star Spangled Banner waved over them. They opened upon us with musketry and artillery. Thick and fast came shot and shell while we returned the compliment in kind. This was war in earnest Standing near Colonel Strange, I heard General A. P. Hill (to whose assistance we had come) say: "Colonel! take two companies from the right of your regiment and charge that battery." My heart sunk within me, for one of those two companies was Company A; but immediately my spirits revived as Colonel Strange replied. "General Hill, I do not recognize your authority as General Pickett is present." All this time the boys were falling to the right and left, and the enemy showing no disposition to leave, General Pickett approached from the right and said: "Advance your regiment at a quick charge when you see the troops on your right move." The battery mentioned was immediately in front of Company A. I was sent down the line to instruct each Captain that the entire brigade would charge at a double quick. I had scarcely reached the left of the regiment, when with a yell that almost drowned the sound of the enemy's guns, Pickett's brigade made its first charge which was but the earnest of its future achievements. Pell-mell we went over logs, through the laps and limbs of the fallen trees, yelling and shooting! on! on! each trying to be a little in advance of the other. Away went the foe—not all, however, for the dead and dying were thick all through that fallen timber. Company A struck the battery and Tom Randolph passing around one end of it and Sergeant Alexander Hoffman passing around the other, they met on the other side and shook hands in token of success. Scarcely had Randolph let go the hand of Hoffman when the latter fell—instantly killed. Thus Company A's first death in battle was one of the bravest of the land. W. T. Jones, John D. Durrett and "Scoff" Vandegrift were thought to be mortally wounded, whilst Wert Murray, Walker Wingfield and William Culin were less seriously hurt.

The battery was ours, however, and Colonel Strange mounted one of the captured horses and rode off to report our capture, but soon returned and reformed the regiment.

The enemy had disappeared, and we marched in the direction of Williamsburg and bivouacked half a mile or more from the scene of action. The killed and wounded mentioned were all members of Company A. Of the wounded W. T. Jones was the only one who was never able to return to duty.

A Funny Accident—Battle
Of Seven Pines

Late in the evening of May 5th, after the battle mentioned in my last, General Pickett requested of Colonel Strange the services of the Adjutant, and I reported for duty at brigade headquarters. I was informed by General Pickett that he had lost sight of the 28th Virginia Regiment, and sent me in search of it. Away I went alone in the direction of the enemy, leaving the battlefield to my left. Going down a hill I came to a small branch, on the south side of which a smooth path was inviting. Riding rapidly down this path (I was horse-back) I observed the branch had become a deep ditch, and soon the ditch became an immense gulley, and yet I must cross it. It was too late in the evening to turn back and take the other side of the branch, and yet my mission would end in failure unless I crossed, for I was evidently going in a wrong direction now. In my dilemma I espied a bridge further down the gulley and hastened to it. The bridge was made of small poles with either end resting on stout logs. I rode upon the bridge and when about half way over the gulley (which was wide and deep) the poles began to roll and the next thing I knew my horse was suspended—all four feet having gone through between the poles. I dismounted with haste and wondered how to extricate the animal from its awkward position. The horse, however, seemed to have no idea of remaining in such an unpleasant situation and began to exert himself, which resulted in his landing safely where I wanted him. Mounting again, off I sped and came up with the Twenty-Eighth in time to save them from capture, for they were going exactly in the wrong direction to find the brigade.

The Nineteenth spent the night southeast of Williamsburg, but marched through the town very early on the morning of the 6th, leaving our badly wounded behind. These poor fellows experienced untold hardships before we saw them again. Vandegrift had the smallpox in prison and has borne ever since the marks of the disease. I have reasons for believing his life was, under Providence, saved by his cheerful disposition and the Sisters of Charity. The same may be said of Jones and Durrett.

Mud, mud, mud! the deepest I ever saw, and the most of it. On the 6th of May, whilst resting on the road, General J. E. Johnston passed us and the boys gave him a rousing cheer. He replied, "That sounds better to me today than it did to the enemy on yesterday," which provoked a real Southern yell.

Marching slowly toward Richmond, we encamped on the south side of the Chickahominy. For three weeks we were occupied in throwing up breastworks, drilling and "running the block" to Richmond, much extra duty resulting from the last mentioned. We changed camp several times during this period, and on Thursday night, May 29th, we were drenched with a heavy rain. A recent removal of camp had caused us to fail to pitch our tents—which, by the way, were articles rapidly growing into disuse.

On Friday extra rations were issued, and in obedience to orders, three days' rations were cooked, and early Saturday morning the regiment took up a line of march toward the enemy. Later in the day everything indicated a fight—firing in front, orderlies riding rapidly, the generals looking solemn and wise, regimental and company officers very strict. We halted for the night not far from Seven Pines and learned that a big fight had taken place that evening and we were "not in it." We had halted in a swamp and there spent the night. I broke off small pines and piled them up until I had a superb bed in the midst of muck and mud. Very few found a place on which to build a fire large enough to set a tin cup in which to make coffee.

Sunday morning, June 1st, dawned upon us clear and warm. About eight o'clock the regiment was formed. Everything was hushed and still. No enemy in sight—no firing; no drums beating. A beautiful, still, quiet, Sabbath morning. "Forward! March!" and we moved lazily down the road and halted on the ground from which the enemy had been whipped the day before. We stacked arms in the road and lounged about with indifference—many of the men picking up trinkets —old letters, packages of ground coffee, bundles of crackers, etc., which had been left by the enemy on the day before. A few tents had been left standing. We were getting to be interested—in fact, were having something of a picnic. I was standing near the head of the stacked arms looking Yankee-wards, when suddenly puffs of smoke arose from the bushes about three hundred yards in front, followed by the report of musketry, whilst here and there the thud of bullets against stumps and the few standing trees brought the picnic to a sudden termination.

The command, "Fall in! fall in!" was given by the adjutant, and in a few minutes a body of well-drilled soldiers was marching toward the bushes from whence came the shots that put an end to the foraging.

General Pickett rode up, and the column was halted and the brigade formed in line of battle. "Forward, March!" "Steady, boys!" "Don't shoot until you see them!" and many similar expressions were used. We had to scramble through the chevaux-de-frise left in place by the enemy the day before and the various obstructions they had used to protect their rear when encamped on our picnic grounds. Marching forward through sharpened pine limbs, through patches of briars, the Nineteenth was stopped suddenly by an immense frog-pond and no enemy in sight. "By the left flank, march!" was the order and we went about two hundred yards to the left, halted, faced to the front and dressed upon the colors. Still no enemy in sight. We were in the edge of a forest—a road just in our rear separating the woods from an old field. "Lie down" was the next order which was cheerfully obeyed. I was standing near the centre of the regiment, far enough in the rear to see the road some distance to the left, and observed troops crossing the road going towards our rear. This I reported to the Colonel, who instructed me to display our flag "as they must be friends." Stepping back and looking again I saw the United States flag, and then knew they were not friends. Approaching the Colonel with this positive information, the tramp, tramp, is distinctly heard in front. The rustling of leaves comes nearer. Blue coats are seen through the bushes, more and more numerous, and coming directly towards us. The click of the minnie is heard as our boys prepare for action, and then the roar of musketry from the two lines of battle breaks upon the Sabbath day. Short, quick and decisive was the work done, the enemy leaving in less than eight minutes at a quick route step. Again inspecting the road, no sign of danger was seen, and to this day I have never learned what became of the troops that crossed the road on our left.

The killed of Company A in this action were James Jones, Marion Pearce, James Collier and William Kidd. Walker Wingfield was wounded again, this time so seriously as not to be able to bear arms again. Coke Wingfield was also severely wounded, and though still living, will ever be a cripple from his wounds. Many others were wounded, the company suffering to the extent of twenty per cent, and what was true of Company A applied to the regiment; on no future occasion was our loss so great in so short a time.

CHAPTER V

Seven Days Near Richmond

After Seven Pines we had nearly four weeks of freedom from fighting. In fact, our duty was comparatively light and rations good. Of course we drilled and did guard duty. Had exercise enough for health and comfort. On the 25th day of June the inevitable three-days' rations order was quietly given the company commandants, and there was rather a suspicion of some stir of some kind, but total ignorance seemed to pervade the camp, and the usual guessing was at a discount. On the morning of the 26th orders arrived very early for light marching. Our haversacks were well-filled, our cartridge-boxes full, and without the least suspicion as to our destiny, the regiment was formed, and then the brigade. Off we moved, leaving the camp in charge of those who were excused from duty by the surgeon.

Skirting around Richmond on the north side we struck

the Mechanicsville pike, which we followed until we could trace the course of the Chickahominy in front and on the right. We halted, and for hours lounged on the side of the road with perfect indifference. The sun reached its zenith, and yet we knew nothing, but as the shadows grew long a distant, but distinct, musketry was heard, and we moved nearer the river and again halted. The firing had come nearer, or certainly sounded more distinct. The seven days' fighting had begun. We lay on our arms that night, and before day on the morning of the 27th crossed the Chickahominy river to find that McClellan's right wing had been doubled up and strong positions were occupied by the Federals.

We marched rapidly down the north side of the river for a few miles and halted near Dr. ———'s residence and stacked arms in a field very near a body of woods in which we rested for an hour or two. I rode alone into an orchard near by and was enjoying the breeze under a large apple-tree when a courtly gentleman, dressed in gray, seemed to be attracted by the same shade, rode up and dismounted. He drew some papers from his pocket and seemed absorbed in them. After awhile he raised his eyes from his papers and said, "Will you ride up to that house and tell Dr. ——— I would be glad to see him here." I quickly obeyed, and returning to the apple-tree, informed the gentleman that the doctor was not at the house.

I joined the boys in the woods, and about half an hour afterwards a courier rode up to General Pickett, who was near us, and requested him to have an envelope, which he handed him, delivered at once to General Lee and General Pickett requested our Colonel to let me take it. Hurriedly mounting my horse I rode on to headquarters as instructed by General Pickett. Imagine my surprise when I approached General Lee to find in him the courtly gentleman whom I met under the apple-tree. I know not what the envelope contained, but the effect was marvelous. Couriers were sent in every direction and when I returned to my command I found it ready to march.

Going eastward we crossed Powhite creek at Gaines' Mill, filed to the right down the creek for some distance until we came to a branch that ran into the creek. Here we filed left and went up the branch and halted near its source. That ominous stillness was observable. Company A was detailed as skirmishers. I was with the regimental and brigade staff who were quietly sitting on their horses just in the rear of the Nineteenth Regiment. I heard some one remark, "Why, what is the matter with Company A?" Looking around I saw the company hesitating to advance (the first and last time) as skirmishers. Dismounting hastily and throwing my bridle reins to an orderly, jumping the branch, I was soon in their midst. "What's the matter, boys?" The response came, "We are ready to go now," and away we went, driving in the skirmish line of the enemy and nearly approaching the top of the hill, when we were ordered to return to the regiment which was at once put in motion—the brigade forming a line of battle that looked formidable. Marching steadily up the hill we received the enemy's fire before reaching the top. The smoke from their guns settled in the bottom between us, and not only concealed the enemy but shut out from view their surroundings. Unfortunately the whole line halted on top of the hill and were raked by the batteries on the south side of the river as well as from those in front. For some time the entire line seemed to hesitate. I was ordered to the left to urge an advance and ran from the right of the regiment to the left of it with the one cry, "Forward! Forward!" and returned about half way to the right when the regiment launched forth into the smoke and dust with a yell which was taken up on either side, and away we went down a steep hill, at the bottom of which was a deep ravine that separated the cleared field through which we came from the body of woods beyond. Nearly exhausted from exertion, I failed to reach the opposite bank of the ravine in attempting to jump it, and found myself at the bottom of a ten-foot ditch, and the boys climbing the hill beyond shouting and shooting like mad. By the time I got out of the ditch the three lines of the enemy's works were in our possession. Of course I felt mean when I overtook the regiment and found no enemy in sight. I had missed what I had often wished to see—the defeat of a cavalry charge on infantry, but was thrilled by the description given me of it by Granville Taylor of Company B. Our loss was heavy. The fighting was the most severe we had experienced. General Pickett was wounded in this, the battle of Gaines' Mill.

CHAPTER VI

Marching Toward
The James

The day after the battle of Gaines' Mill we crossed to the south side of the Chickahominy and marched toward James river and got thoroughly drenched in the rain.

The 29th of June was clear, however, and somehow there was unusual quiet as we delayed on the road side waiting seemingly for something to "turn up." The sun was declining when a distant gun was heard and we marched rapidly down the road in a wooded country, halted and formed a line of battle in the road with our backs toward James river. The manœuver indicated that we had surrounded somebody and were now ready to bag the game. "Forward, march!" was the command and leaving the road behind us, we entered the forest to find ourselves in a bramble thicket, with hawthorns and wild roses interlocked. A little further on we were in water and slush, and again a little further, something did "turn up" (in the shape of a pretty line of blue coats), just as we emerged from the woods, and it took several volleys of musketry to drive them away. We did drive them, however, and followed them across the field until late at night. Darkness put an end to the fight. William Culin and Tom Frank Wingfield were killed in this (Frasier's farm) fight and Henry Lorsh was severely wounded. Others of Company A suffered from bruises and slight wounds.

On the 30th we seemed to be in search of something lost. We marched through bushes and briars, along unused paths, across bogs and branches but found nothing except the leavings of the rapid-going enemy.

July 1st we approached Malvern Hill, but were not called upon to take a hand, though exposed to those miserable nail-keg missiles from the enemy's gun-boats in the James. In passing around Malvern Hill, July 2d, we observed many signs of a terrific conflict. In a body of old field pines, through which we passed, every tree seemed to have been struck by many bullets or shells. It was here that Colonel Strange said: "Men! have I not told you it was dangerous to seek shelter behind a tree? Look! every pine was struck." A piping voice from the ranks was heard: "Yes, Colonel, them pines stopped a heap of bullets."

We followed McClellan to his "safe retreat" and had several days of easy life in regular camp duty. We remained here long enough to recruit the regiment considerably. Many of the slightly wounded returned to duty and many absentees came in.

Richmond was safe. We knew we had an army of *soldiers* and a general worthy of the men he commanded. Why did McClellan not take Richmond? I almost quote the *Examiner* of that day when I say, because there was a Pickett to pass, two Hills to cross, rough Rodes to overcome, a Longstreet to travel and a Strange by path across the Gulley (ordnance officer of the Nineteenth Virginia).

On the 12th or 13th of August we took the train in Richmond and were landed at Gordonsville later in the day, going into camp in Louisa county not far from Bowler's Mill. On our way from Gordonsville to camp, we passed the Seventh Virginia Infantry which had preceded us long enough to locate comfortably. Passing near Captain McMullen's company from Green county, in which the writer had several acquaintances, one of them hailed me and said, "Just got a box from home; so you must take dinner with me." It was about 3 o'clock, and the invitation was accepted without a repetition. Fried chicken, old ham, apple pies, etc., were set before me. "Hold up a minute. Try this before you begin." "No, thank you, I never drink anything," was the reply, as a canteen was offered. "It is nothing but innocent cherry bounce—why it would not hurt a baby," with which assurance a good hearty pull was taken from the canteen. It was good—in fact, so very palatable was this cherry bounce that a second hearty pull was taken before due attention was paid to the other contents of the box. Eating and talking consumed about thirty minutes and Big I arose to go—or rather he tried to, for somehow the trees seemed to be dancing, the men around the box wonderfully mixed up— the tongue was thick, the knees weak, the head whirling and the leafy shade inviting; all because cherry bounce was innocent. "All present or *accounted for*" at roll call that evening.

This encampment near Bowler's Mill was one of the most pleasant now recalled. Short and sweet was the stay, however, for we struck tents about the 17th of August and went in search of the boastful Pope. Marching northward we crossed the Rapidan near the station of the same name and followed the railroad for some distance, but moved eastward before arriving at Culpeper Courthouse, returning to the railroad by

Stephensburg, near which place it was reported a spy was caught in our lines and duly hung.

John Llewellyn had received the appointment of Adjutant and I returned to my duty in the company. We approached the Rappahannock river and were greeted with shells from the northern side. We made several demonstrations and frequently occupied conspicuous positions, evidently to let the enemy know where we were. In one of those conspicuous positions four of our poker-players stretched a blanket by "putting on" the bayonet and sticking them in the ground, and then catching each corner of the blanket in the lock of the musket, a shade was secured for the game. It is thought the enemy concluded this impromptu tent was headquarters as they viewed it through their glasses, and took extra pains to bring a long-range piece of artillery to bear upon it. Their aim was good, for a solid shot came whistling through the air, barely missing the absorbed players without doing more damage than breaking up the game. Moving leisurely up the Rappahannock we crossed near Jeffersonton to the north side and struck a bee line at a quick step towards Jackson's position near Manassas.

CHAPTER VII

Second Battle Of
Manassas

With quickened step we hurried through the dust, which was excessive. With parched lips we anxiously looked for springs and wells by the roadside. From each company a number of men were detailed to take ten or twelve canteens and hurry forward and have them filled by the time the regiment came up. The August sun was scorching hot. Rumors as to General Jackson's safety were current, and something of uneasiness seemed to pervade the entire command as we hurried through Fauquier county and into Prince William. The sun was sinking in the west as we approached Thoroughfare Gap and halted on the Manassas gap railroad on August 28th, 1862. The commandants of companies were instructed to avoid making a noise, and fires were prohibited. As night came on we went a little further in the Gap, but as silently as if attending a funeral. Talking was done almost in a whisper, and the tread was nigh unto silent. Every man was cautioned to remain in his place as we halted, and there was no breaking ranks. The cold bread and beef were eaten, and thus "in place rest" we spent the night. Looking backward out of the deep cut no one would be convinced that nearly all of Longstreet's corps were reposing in that immediate vicinity. The morning dawned and with it came the orders "Forward," and we passed through the Gap.

Marching rapidly from Thoroughfare Gap on the morning of the 29th (August 1862), we heard artillery off to the left. Going eastward some miles, we halted not far south of the battlefield of July 21, 1861. We stacked arms and broke ranks, having received orders not to wander off. We had about six hours of real quiet—nothing to disturb or molest us. About four o'clock p.m. the regiment was formed in a line of battle and remained in line for nearly an hour. There was nothing in sight to alarm, though the firing away off to the left had increased and come nearer. "Attention! Forward, march!" and with steady step the Nineteenth went forward. Company A was on the right of the regiment and Sergeant James Perley was on the right of Company A. The command was "Dress on the colors," they being in the centre. We marched some distance and no foe appeared. It was getting monotonous as we passed through the pasturefield, and the scene reminded me of an old hare hunt on Christmas—each man seemed to expect an old hare to bounce forward at any moment. "Sergeant Perley, dress to the left," but Perley was too busy looking for his old hare to hear the command, while the gap between him and the regiment continued to widen. "Sergeant Perley! dress to the left!" was again thundered by the company commandant, but still Perley heard not, but branching off further to the right, seemed determined to form an independent army of his own. The officer made a jump or two and was quickly by the side of the little Sergeant, when he threw his left hand in front to attract or arouse. The left hand happened to fall upon the collar of the wanderer who turned red in the face and there and then was ready to leave off fighting the enemy and fight any man who dared to put his hand in his collar. Peace was quickly restored, however, and each took his place in the line of battle which continued a forward march, getting into a cornfield, where we halted and expected every minute to meet the foe. We remained in this position for several hours without suffering more inconvenience than that caused by the Lieutenant Colonel's horse breaking and rushing madly down the line and bruising one or two men. We returned to our bivouac before midnight, and spent the remainder of the night in peaceful slumber. The next day, August 30th, was a lovely day. The morning was so still and quiet that everybody seemed to be on his good behavior.

Our regiment shifted position in the morning, thereby getting nearer the water. It seemed that we were on Longstreet's right and possibly would not be called into action. We wrote letters and smoked. We ate our midday meal and smoked. Some slept beneath the shade of the banks of the branch. "Boys, is not that musketry we hear way off to the left?" And we listened. An orderly dashes up to the Colonel's rock. The command to fall in is given by the commandants of companies. The regiment is formed. The brigade is formed— yea, the division is formed, and the whole line moves forward. The firing has come nearer, much nearer; the artillery is heard not far to the left. The command came, "Forward!" and a magnificent line of veterans—for we were veterans even at this early day—marched to the conflict. Through a skirt of woods we went and emerged on the northern side to witness a scene that has been remembered ever since. Near us, but a little to our left, was a residence. Two hundred yards in front, or a little to the left of our front, was a hill on which the enemy had artillery, well protected by infantry. In front the foe seemed inclined to receive us warmly. A hasty glance convinced us that work was at hand. The hill was the objective point, as from it came grape and shell, sending many a poor Confederate to the ground. Being in command of the company my time was occupied, but the grandeur of the scene was not entirely lost. The lone star of the Texas boys was approaching the hill to our left with steady step and unflinching mien. We were flanking the hill and driving the enemy from our front. Captain Deering, on the right, was splitting the wind as he charged with his battery. Unlimbering, wheeling, firing, limbering up, dashing forward and again in action. The hill was gallantly defended, and it was only when the impetuous, yelling, dashing Confederates had nearly surrounded the hill that the enemy broke and fled, their own guns being used upon them to hasten their going. John LeTellier worked a gun with good effect. A second grand victory upon the plains of Manassas within a period of fourteen months and the position of the armies reversed. Company A lost William Johnston, killed, and many wounded. Among the latter was R. C. Vandergrift. That gallant officer, Charley Peyton, of Company E, lost an arm and David Goodman, of Company B, lost a leg.

First Maryland
Campaign

We left the plains of Manassas August 31st, and when Teltow struck up "Maryland, My Maryland," a shout went up from the Nineteenth which proved the popularity of a Northern tour upon which dame rumor said we were entering. Crossing Bull Run we headed towards Washington, marching over ground that had been familiar to us. We barely missed the fight at Ox Hill, on September 1st, but got wet as rats in the storm that lent its aid to the occasion. We soon passed away from the haunts of the previous winter and found ourselves marching through the county of Loudoun. Officers were scarce. Many of them were at home or in hospitals, sick or wounded. The companies had been much reduced by the casualties of war, and in some instances two companies were thrown into one temporarily, in order to have a commissioned officer to command. Companies A and I had been thus merged into one company for a few days during our march through Loudoun, and the writer placed in command.

The following incident is related to show how strict were the orders during this invasion. For some reason our command was very late going into camp on the night of September 4th. It was pitch dark, and the march was slow. I was informed that Colonel Strange wished to see me at the head of the column. I approached him and made my presence known. "Lieutenant, did you not hear the orders about straggling?" "I did, sir." "One of the men under your command has just been discovered ahead of his company. Consider yourself under arrest." "All right, sir," and the interview ended.

We went into camp for the night a few minutes afterwards. Early the next morning I was aroused by the Adjutant who informed me that the Colonel sent compliments and wished me to resume my duties. My reply was: "Present my compliments to the Colonel and inform him that I question his right to put me under arrest for the offense mentioned, and therefore decline to resume my duties, and demand a court of inquiry." Thus, as a gentleman of leisure, I crossed the Potomac at White's Ford with the command on the 5th of September, and joined in the shout as we struck Maryland soil. We proceeded to the bridge of the Baltimore and Ohio railway, over the Monocacy, and went into camp. Here we enjoyed for several days the ease and quiet of camp-life.

Our most excellent commissary, Major H. W. Jones (may his useful life be long spared), had us well supplied with bread and meat, and I am sure our quartermaster, Major George T. Jones, would have been glad to supply us with uniforms becoming visitors in a strange land. But he could not—hence the army presented anything but a military appearance, except in deportment and accoutrements. The boys would take care of their arms; and, with pride I write, the great mass of Confederates were gentlemen. At this camp

(Monocacy) General R. B. Garnett assumed command of our brigade.

We made visits to Frederick in small squads, and I recall a supper that I enjoyed with a family, each one of whom exhibited a Confederate flag with becoming grace.

On Thursday, September 11th, we struck tents—so-called —and began our march westward, passing through the Blue Ridge near Boonsboro, arriving at Hagerstown on Saturday, the 13th. It was on this march that we so often passed large crowds who had assembled on the roadside to see the show of a Southern army. In one crowd was a large, well-dressed woman, standing very near the road. She had pinned on her breast a beautiful and attractive United States flag. Of course the wag and wit of the company could not allow such an opportunity to pass unimproved, so stepping almost out of ranks, and making a polite bow as he halted near her, said: "We are in the habit of charging breastworks wherever we see that flag floating," and resumed his position in line.

We had begun to make ourselves comfortable at Hagerstown when a distant rumbling on Sunday morning was heard. Listening attentively convinced us that trouble was brewing some distance in the rear. The inevitable courier appeared. The regiment was formed and we entered upon a forced march over the road we had so recently trod. By four o'clock we were climbing the mountain east of Boonsboro, and it was then not difficult to learn the object in view. We had come to aid the small force of D. H. Hill in resisting the passage of the mountain gap by McClellan. Arriving on top of the mountain we prepared for action. Just a little east of the top (on the Frederick side) we formed a line of battle in the road, mounted the fence and entered a stubble field and advanced in the line of battle. Several pieces of artillery opened upon us from the mountain side off to our right, and suddenly we received a heavy fire from the front. We were dreadfully exposed to the cross fire while the enemy was concealed behind a rock fence in our front. Some one gave the command "charge" and at them we went, but were recalled before getting possession of the entire fence. Orders came to fall back to the road, and we did so in good order, waiting for and expecting the enemy to advance. They did not, however, and after dark we moved down the western slope of the mountain and spent the remainder of the night. The object had been accomplished. McClellan had failed to force his way through the mountain in time to save Harper's Ferry, and "Mars Bob" had gained all the time he wanted to mass his troops at Sharpsburg.

In this Boonsboro affair Company A lost the gallant Tom Randolph (see University Memorial) and J. J. Christian, killed on the spot. It was here that Colonel John Bowie Strange was killed. Company B lost the Sheppard boys—Mell and Dan—rich sacrifices to a sacred memory. Again it seemed the noblest and best had fallen. It was in this fight that J. M. Brown of Company F received the wound that gave rise to the name—"One-Arm Brown."

CHAPTER IX

The Battle Of
Sharpsburg

The death of Colonel Strange put an end to the court of inquiry, and on the morning of Monday, September 15th, I assumed command of the company, and returned to regular duty—having been foolish enough to go into the battle of Boonsboro on something of an independent style.

Arriving at Sharpsburg during the day Monday, we passed around the town and bivouacked on the south side. Upon investigating our haversacks we found rations getting scarce, and as we had nothing else to do on Tuesday but to eat, we were without rations that evening. This must be explained. In returning to Boonsboro on Sunday the 14th, we left our wagons at Hagerstown. Instructions were given quartermasters, commissaries and officers of surplus ordnance not to follow us, but to proceed to cross the Potomac at some convenient place and wait for the troops, hence when the troops halted at Sharpsburg several miles intervened between troops and rations.

On the morning of Wednesday, September 17th, our brigade marched around the town on the east side at an early hour; spent half an hour listening near a large spring, which I located from memory on the northeast suburbs of the town. By nine o'clock we had formed a line of battle on the north side of the town—the right of the brigade not far in front of the spring. Suddenly a shell came whistling over the high hill in our front, and though the infantry made no display of their meagre lines and the artillery was very limited, this shell was followed by the heaviest artillery fire from the enemy's guns that I had up to that time ever heard, and save one single occasion, the heaviest I ever witnessed. For an hour, possibly, we remained behind the hill and out of sight; but as those immense projectiles came "swapping ends" over the hill, our brigade commander discovered that we would be safer nearer the top, and advanced the line accordingly. Advancing to the top and hurriedly glancing across the Antietam, I was impressed as never before with the bigness of war. For miles in something of a semi-circle the enemy had batteries of heavy guns planted on every hill, commanding our position, and it seemed that every gun opened every minute. The smoke rolled backward to the mountains in their rear, but their destructive shot and shell were falling, it would appear, on every foot of land behind us. They were shooting over us. I think they supposed this hill was strongly defended and that their heavy firing was playing havoc with us. The truth of the matter was we had here little else than the hill—a battery of four guns, and a brigade of infantry so reduced by the casualties of war that, in order to cover the ground, it had to deploy at least six feet apart. I doubt not that at one time there was one piece of artillery firing at the hill to every five men we had defending it.

Towards the middle of the day there was a lull in the storm and we expected to see their infantry advance, but for some unaccountable reason they advanced but a short distance and did not come within the range of our muskets. In fact, they did not cross the creek of Antietam. In the afternoon they began anew, with better aim, and for hours, it seemed, poured shot and shell into our decimated ranks. One continuous roar of cannon and an ever-enlarging cloud of smoke, banking against the mountain in their rear. The sun was declining and we wished for night, for of all mean things the climax is reached when compelled to receive the fury of cannonading with no opportunity to inflict damage. Here we were, nothing to do but patiently to await events.

Soon, however, a heavy column of infantry crossed the creek and exposed itself to our artillery. Off on our right a heavy column had reached our thin line, which was just beginning to retire, when timely aid arrived from Harper's Ferry which sent the enemy rolling back whence they came. Would the same aid reach our brigade in time? Onward came the immense column of well-drilled infantry. Our battery was reduced to two guns, but these were worked by cool, brave men, who loaded with rapidity and sent canister thick and fast into the approaching ranks. Now they were within range of our muskets, and every musket did its duty. The few officers we had sheathed the sword and joined in the deadly conflict with muskets. On they came with slow but steady tread. Filling up the gaps we made in their ranks, they seemed determined to take the hill. They wavered for an instant, as rapid discharges of grape mowed great openings in their ranks. They closed up again, however, and approached nearer. No time to look for the wished-for assistance—impossible to wait for them. General Garnett gave the order to retire, and with one more round at very short range, we left the hill where, for eight hours, we had been exposed to the fury of a mighty host.

As the brigade of about two hundred and fifty men yielded the hill to eight times their number, we felt that more could not be expected of us. But the hill? We had just left when aid arrived, and in five minutes sent that mighty throng down the hill with more haste than characterized their approach. The hill was still ours. In this engagement the writer commanded the regiment and was aided most heartily and efficiently by Lieutenant James Grinstead of Company K, no other commissioned officer of the entire regiment being present.

Our regiment had numbered eight hundred. On this occasion we had only fifty-four. Our brigade had numbered more than three thousand, on this occasion we had about two hundred and fifty. Why was this? Simply because we had received no absentees since entering Maryland, but were daily depleted by sickness, and the usual casualties of battle and marches.

Our regiment did not return to the hill that night but formed a nucleus in the rear for all the stragglers to be found, and by nine o'clock we had a supporting column of one thousand tried men, many of whom arrived that evening from the Virginia side of the Potomac—this being the first opportunity they had for two weeks, to rejoin their commands. On the morning of the 18th our brigade returned to the hill with nearly double the number of the previous day. The Army of Northern Virginia defiantly invited a renewal of the attack but it came not, and on the night of the 18th and morning of 19th, crossed the Potomac near Shepherdstown and thus ended the campaign.

CHAPTER X

The Shooting Of A Deserter
—Battle Of Gettysburg

About the first of June, 1863, we left our camp at Anderson's and went to Tappahannock, returning on the third. Remained two days, and marched to Culpeper, where we encamped one week. A new battle-flag was presented to the regiment at Culpeper by the government, and the old one, now in Jim Perley's possession, was sent to the rear. We left Culpeper on the 14th and marched northward, crossing the Blue Ridge at Snicker's gap on the 17th. On the 18th we waded the Shenandoah, but crossed back the next day and showed ourselves to the enemy on the mountain. Waded the Shenandoah again that evening and joined the corps near Berryville on the 19th or 20th. Here we rested two or three days. On the 25th we crossed the Potomac near Williamsport and were again in Maryland.

Here, the day we crossed the river, I witnessed for the first time the shooting of a deserter. The brigade formed three sides of a square and the prisoner was placed on the fourth side on his knees, his hands tied behind him near his coffin. A detail of twelve men, commanded by a commissioned officer, was placed opposite the doomed man. One-half of the muskets contained a ball each, the other half had powder only. Not one of the detail knew whether or not his gun contained a ball. Each man was instructed to aim at the breast. The word "fire" was given and the poor unfortunate received six bullets—four of them could have been covered with a half a sheet of note paper, and the two not far off. The effect was beneficial to other substitutes, whose only object it was to secure the pay and desert.

That night we rested in Maryland, and the next day entered Pennsylvania and arrived at Chambersburg on the 27th. Orders were strict and rigidly enforced. There were but few stragglers—almost none. Public and private property was not molested except by due process of military law, and the men were orderly and polite.

The following incident, which occurred in Chambersburg, is characteristic. The division Chief Commissary of Subsistence (Major H. W. Jones) ascertained that in a large cellar in the town was a quantity of stores, much needed by our division. Upon consultation with the proprietor of the establishment, it was agreed that they go together and set apart certain articles to be called for by our wagons. They entered the cellar by themselves, but soon from hidden nooks, friends (possibly United States soldiers) of the proprietor joined them. They first became impertinent, then insulting, and finally threatening. Major Jones was not armed—had trusted the proprietor and expected nothing but a courteous business transaction. The Major remonstrated at the proceedings, and I suspect was in more danger than he realized. His movements had brought the crowd near a grating, opening into the street. Near the grating were two Confederates, who, attracted by the noise, quickly pulled up the iron frame and in the nick of time, stood with fixed bayonets by the side of the Major, who, taking in the situation, cleared the cellar at the point of the bayonet, first of the proprietor and his friends, and afterwards of everything that could be used by the soldiers.

On the morning of July 2d our brigade hastened towards Gettysburg. The rank and file knew nothing of the fight then in progress, but from the activity of our movements a few guesses were made as to the near future. Arriving in the vicinity of Gettysburg on the evening of the same day, we gathered some information as to what had been going on. We bivouacked that night about three miles from the scene of action of the 1st and 2d without being disturbed by the nearness of the battlefield. Early in the morning of the 3d we prepared and ate our frugal meal. The usual jests and hilarity were indulged in, and soon after, when ordered into line, and we again took up the march, no gloomy forebodings hovered over our ranks. We marched possibly three miles and gradually approached the enemy. A shady, quiet march was this, protected from the enemy's view by woods and Cemetery Hill. We halted for a short time in the woods, but moved forward pretty soon into a field, near a branch. Here we filled our canteens and took things easy for twenty minutes, or possibly longer. Up to this time our march had been in column, but our next move was in line of battle to the front—halting immediately after crossing a road and getting over the fence on either side of the road. Remaining in this position but a few minutes, we moved forward again, and this time as we halted we dressed upon the colors, forming a line of battle. The other regiments of our brigade dressed upon us—ours being the centre regiment. We were ordered to lie down. Our position was, at this time, on the south side of Cemetery Hill and near its eastern end, and less than a hundred yards from the top in our front.

For how many hours we sweltered on the side of this hill that hot third day of July, 1863, I know not, but my own opinion is about five hours.

The field-officers rode about us and held frequent short consultations. Leaving my command I walked up to the top of the hill and took a birds-eye view of the situation, just as Colonel Deering rode up to see about locating his artillery. I heard him say "that hill must fall" as he rode off to the right. I walked back to the regiment with "that hill must fall" ringing in my ears. Artillery came, it seemed to me, from every direction, and quickly prepared, on or near the hill top, for action. I never before saw such a display of artillery and felt, "that hill must fall."

An hour or more passed in silence. The sun was making the hillside very uncomfortable. Activity among the artillery men was observed, the word "fire" was heard, more than one hundred guns opened the fight. The enemy replied at once. The earth seemed to leap from its foundation; the atmosphere seemed to quiver, the smoke rose in balloon-shape and gently drifted to the left. The sun's heat was forgotten and mother-earth embraced with a soldier's ardour. The shells, bursting over and behind us, sent missiles upon any one who might be lurking in the rear. Again the enemy was overshooting the mark and doing but little damage to the infantry. From Roundtop, two miles to our right came those miserable enfilading solid shots which frequently struck the ground on our right, ricochetting along the line to the death and injury of many. Lieutenant-Colonel John T. Ellis was lying in a small wash on the hillside, as one of those balls came bounding from the right. Some one hollowed—"look out" and he raised his head just in time to receive the ball in his face. Kind friends bore him to the shade, where death eased him of all pain. In Colonel Ellis we lost a good officer, a good man as well as a polished gentleman.

CHAPTER XI

The Charge At Gettysburg

How long this terrific cannonading lasted I know not, but it did cease. "Attention!" was heard along the infantry line, and every man sprang to his feet, and then was observed a singular excitement. All along the line men were falling from seeming sunstroke with dreadful contortions of the body, foaming at the mouth, and almost lifeless. Some were possibly shamming but much, real, downright suffering from the sun's hot rays was experienced. But why this effect just as they rose and felt the breeze? They were taken to the shade and order restored in the ranks. "Forward, guide centre, march!" and we moved forward to the top of the hill—just in front of our artillery, and halted. Here we formed a beautiful line of battle and were in full view of the enemy. Glancing my eyes over the field I felt, "That hill must fall" still applied to the future. Forward again! and, look yonder! Kemper's brigade in splendid array, moving steadily forward. To the left and rear is Armistead's brigade seemingly more hurried as they come into line. What a line of battle! How they keep together! "That hill must fall." Onward we move in common marching time. No excitement. No loud commands. "Steady, boys," "Don't fire," "Close up," "Never mind the skirmish line," as that of the enemy hastened to shelter. Over the plain we marched. Surely the hill has fallen. No, look! They are bringing fresh artillery to bear upon us. Again the shrieking shot and bursting shell, and now the blazing musketry. Forward, still forward. How thin the ranks are getting. Down the gradual descent we hurry. Over the fence we scramble. We bound diagonally across the Emmetsburg Pike and feel that the hill has fallen.

Just beyond the Emmetsburg pike was the bottom, the greatest depression between the two armies. The bottom was speedily reached and up Cemetery Hill we start. Grape and canister scour the ground. Down! down! go the boys. The remainder press forward. The enemy's line—a stone and dirt wall—is just in front. Suddenly the firing in our front ceases and the brave boys renew their efforts to reach the goal. Just then, when within twenty yards of the rock fence, I received a blow on the right leg. Am I wounded? Leaning against a rock, I ascertain it to be only a bruise, and again went forward with the small remnant. Stopping at the fence, I looked to the right and left and felt we were disgraced. Where were those who started in the charge? With one single exception I witnessed no cowardice, and yet we had not a skirmish line. Less than two hundred yards to my right the enemy was forming a line of battle on our side of the fence. Their right was at the fence, their left was being rapidly extended into the field to our rear. I watched them as they began to move in our direction. To remain was life in prison. To retreat was probable death in crossing the field, but possible safety within our lines, and without a moment's hesitation I turned my back to the fence and started across that nearly three quarters of a mile over which we had so recently come. Warm, tired and thirsty I limped down the hill, and felt like taking shelter behind a pile of rails that lay invitingly in my way just as the enemy opened upon us again. Resisting the temptation, I was walking rapidly when a twinge in the side and a ball of wadding from my coat and vest caused me to think a ball had gone through me. I slackened my speed and expected every second to feel the blood trickling down. At last I reached our line and hastened to the shade. The first voice I heard was that of Lucien Jones, asking if I thought my wound serious. My reply was, "I think I am shot through," and asked his condition. He replied, "I am mortally wounded, but fell in the discharge of duty and near the cannon's mouth." He died the next day. I immediately entered upon an investigation of my injuries. Removing my coat I observed it was much torn by the ball. My vest was also torn in front. With intense anxiety and bated breath I removed my shirt and found there the same evidences of a musket ball's reckless speed. I also observed blood stains as I dropped it on the ground. Further investigation revealed a scratch only.

In returning across the field between the lines, I saw enough to account readily for the thin line that reached the much-talked of stone fence, and when General Pickett silently extended his hand, and as he turned aside almost sobbed out the words, "My brave men! My brave men!" I felt that after all we were not disgraced.

The men were easily rallied, and a line of battle formed for any emergency. We had, for the first time, failed to do what we attempted, but the earnestness of the effort was attested by the great loss sustained. Our brigade commander, General R. B. Garnett, was killed near the enemy's line. He went into action on horseback, not being able to walk. He was a noble specimen of manhood and was greatly admired by those who knew him. His memory is perpetuated in my household by my youngest child bearing his name. Our regimental losses were as follows: Henry Gantt, colonel, wounded early in action, escaped and recovered; John T. Ellis, lieutenant-colonel, killed as mentioned. Our major, Charles Peyton, went to the rock fence and returned without injury. Acting Adjutant James D. McIntire was badly wounded but escaped capture. The officers of Company A were three in number and fared as follows: Captain John C. Culin, as usual, was wounded, but escaped capture; Lieutenant Wood, slightly wounded; Lieutenant John Hill, captured and died in prison. Sergeant James R. Buck and Corporal George Thomas Johnson were captured, but not wounded. Privates John D. Durrett badly wounded and William M. Dudley and James H. Dudly captured; John A. Bowen killed; John W. Houchens wounded and captured; Polk Points wounded but escaped. Two or three more whose names are not mentioned were missing. The company was small, indeed, the next morning as an effort was made to get the men together. Major Peyton was senior officer of the regiment—fit for duty—if not of the brigade.

The day after the fight was spent in an attitude of defiance by the army. Toward its close, however, our brigade moved southward a few miles and halted for the night. Nearly five thousand prisoners were placed in the custody of Pickett's command in the retreat. These prisoners expected to be recaptured before we reached the Potomac, and many of them spoke of Meade's delay in doing so. Being in command of the guard a good portion of the time, I mingled freely with them, discussing everything except politics. They seemed much surprised at courtesies extended them and were loud in praising their guard. Upon our arrival at or near Williamsport on the 7th we found our retreat hindered by high water. The army was placed in position for fighting, but the enemy seemed too tired to attack. For four days we were ready to receive them, but not until the entire army of Northern Virginia crossed over into Virginia were there any demonstrations. Our regiment crossed, I think on the 13th. The prisoners were turned over to other troops on the 16th after we passed through Winchester, and I returned to my command near Bunker Hill.

The Cat Wouldn't Cook Done

Our stay in the Valley was short. The return of absentees swelled the companies of our regiment into fair proportions. In fact, when called upon to hurry across the Shenandoah River to protect a mountain pass, and keep the gap clear of the enemy, who made a movement threatening to bottle us up in the Valley, the regiment made a good show, and proved that good material was yet in the ranks. We encamped one night near White Post, in Clarke county, and as usual on a march, the camp was quiet at an early hour. During the night a sudden rushing sound was heard. The rapid tread of beasts, the breaking of sticks and brush, as well as the dust, forced the conclusion that the cavalry of the enemy was upon us. We were in a beautiful oak grove, and instinctively each man sought a tree or rock—some with arms and not a few without—some clothed and in their right minds, and some otherwise. The entire camp was aroused, but before military order prevailed, it was ascertained that a lot of cattle had by some means been stampeded and with an "Oh, pshaw!" the men again retired to rest.

We left the Valley about July 20, and made our way by short marches to Culpeper Courthouse where we remained about a week. Early in August we crossed to the south side of the Rapidan and went in to camp near Somerville Ford. We remained in Orange county until the 8th day of September, 1863, when we pulled up stakes for Chaffin's Farm, about seven miles east of Richmond. As we approached Chaffin's, we met a portion of General Henry A. Wise's brigade, whose position we were to occupy. Here we found the most comfortable quarters we had occupied during the war. The men of Wise's brigade had occupied these quarters for a long period, and made themselves decidedly comfortable—judging from what we saw in turnip-patches and other evidences of gardening. They had cows and chickens and were living at home, as our boys expressed it. Good log houses with bunks, and wide fireplaces, and brick hearths in some instances, were luxuries unknown to us for many months. How much we enjoyed this new phase in soldiering can be neither told nor imagined. Furloughs were granted as rapidly as circumstances would admit. Permission to visit the capital of the Confederacy was systematically arranged. Every man ordered his best suit from home (provided he had one). "Blockade running" to Richmond was a thing of daily occurrence. Many of the few married men in the regiment secured quarters nearby for their wives. Ladies frequently appeared at our dress parades. Parties in the vicinity became a weekly affair. The violin and banjo appeared in camp. What a jolly winter was that of 1863-4 to the men of Hunton's brigade! Rations became very scarce, however, and but for the boxes from home such a delicacy as hog meat would have been almost unknown. There was suffering in Richmond, and well do I remember how unanimous was the voice in camp, to spare a portion of our limited meat-rations for the benefit of the needy of the Capitol City.

Among the many home-like legacies left us by the brigade of General Wise was a large cat. This cat looked so fat and slick, that the idea of making a dinner of her was suggested by a Captain of the regiment, who said: "What nice venison she will make." The cat was slaughtered and nicely dressed and put in a camp kettle to cook. All day the cat boiled and at every trial to stick in the fork to ascertain when tender, the report was "not done yet." "Lights out" came and still the cat was not tender. Carefully the camp kettle was set aside for the night and next morning the effort to cook the cat was resumed. The mess quietly indulged in a game of "old sledge" and patiently watched the boiling kettle, but the cat still resisted the fork. Finally, late in the evening of the second day's cooking and waiting it was decided, "Let us eat her anyhow." The mess gathered around the table and Captain Charles ———— undertook to carve. "What is the matter with this knife, Dick?" "Nothing in the world the matter with the knife; it is that darn'd old cat we have been boiling for two days." And it was a correct conclusion; for no knife was found that would cut that "venison" and the dinner was spoiled.

The writer of these reminiscences was at home, about seven miles north of Charlottesville, on a furlough, about the first of March, 1864, when rumors of a raid by the enemy's cavalry were reported by some school children. I had on a new Confederate uniform, made conspicuous by new buttons and tinsel. Taking a carbine in my hand, I walked out to ascertain the facts of the rumored raid. I struck the public road at the intersection of the Crank road, not far south of the present residence of W. H. Bowcock, and leisurely walked northward. The road being nearly straight, I could see some distance towards Mayo's shop. A solitary cavalryman was approaching, who, from general appearance, I recognized as a United States soldier. We were slowly approaching each other, when he, descending a small hill near the Campbell house, was lost to sight. I embraced this opportunity to get over the high stake fence on my right and felt no regret at seeing him ascending the hill and retracing his steps at full speed.

Being satisfied a raiding party was near, and wishing to ascertain more definitely as to numbers and movements, I hurried through the woods to the Rio road and arrived near the "stone culvert" in time to learn that the command was large and marching towards the town of Charlottesville. Hurrying home I joined James H. Burnley just as his plowman (John Southall, who now lives near Hydraulic) came dashing up on a strange horse and exclaiming, "The soldiers have taken my horses." "What horses?" "John Rattler and ———" Mr. Burnley immediately had his remaining horses—about fifteen—hurried through a gateway and over the barn hill to the woods near the river. He and many servants went with them. He owned about one hundred servants at that time. Just as I joined the crowd on the barn hill I saw a cavalryman approaching the residence of my father, about two hundred yards north of the residence of J. H. Burnley's. I remarked if I had a horse I would pay my respects to the visitor. A Mr. Ellis standing near replied: "There is my horse—you are welcome to him." I rode down the barn hill, through the gateway, through the stable-lot and up the hill towards my father's residence. As I approached the house, the lone cavalryman rode from one end of the yard to the other, watching my zig-zag course. Finally we faced each other, separated by the yard. I raised my carbine, and he leveled his pistol. A number of the enemy's cavalrymen in the road about two hundred yards off were watching us, and fired upon me just as my friend across the yard and myself emptied our pieces at each other. He wheeled and rode rapidly off. I wheeled, but my horse was so badly hurt that my movements were slow. Retracing my steps down the hill, through the lots, and through the gateway, I started up the barn hill. My horse had come down to a slow walk and the enemy were charging down the lane, and almost intercepted me at the gateway. Here they halted, and as my horse slowly climbed the hill, I turned in my saddle and hallooed, "Come on." They seemed to count the horsetracks in the gateway and evidently concluded an ambush was set for them, and followed me no further. I passed over the hill, and just as I dismounted, my horse fell dead. The enemy rode into Mr. Burnley's yard, made a few enquiries, and one of them showed a considerable rent in his coat, which he said was made by my bullet. They did no damage and soon left the neighborhood.

C H A P T E R   X I I I

Off To The Front Again

Upon my return to camp, from a short stay at home on furlough, I found the regiment on a bleak hillside, north of Richmond, suffering all the ills of March winds and out-of-door log fires. The smoke was awful. The regiment had been called out to protect the city from the Dahlgren raiders who managed to come to grief without the aid of the Nineteenth. We speedily returned to our snug quarters at Chaffin's farm and spent the remainder of March in blissful ease and comfort.

During the month of April we made a few hurried trips to different places to strengthen weak points, but without coming in contact with the enemy. With the month of May came all sorts of rumors, as to movements of the enemy and our service. We had become so proud of our Gettysburg glory that we were content to hold the important point of Chaffin's farm to the end of the chapter. This was not to be, however, for one bright May morning—the 8th, I think it was—we received orders to prepare rations and get ready for light marching. Away went all surplus baggage to Richmond, speedily followed by the regiment. Passing through the city on the north side we bivouacked near the Brook turnpike. On the 9th we marched westward a short distance, then eastward, and before night we went northward. Rain began to fall and we longed for the slab-roof huts at Chaffin's.

On the 10th we hurried in the direction of Yellow Tavern and soon heard the old familiar sound of artillery. Entering a piece of woods at a double quick we were saluted by shells from an unseen foe—one shell passing through the woods, burst almost in the midst of Company A, but without doing more damage than throwing mud and water upon the men. We had not the opportunity of engaging the enemy—the entire fight being that of cavalry. General Stuart fell in this fight, mortally wounded, and many a cavalryman fought his last battle on this memorable day.

News from the Wilderness reached us, and we expected orders to march to the front, but, to our surprise and delight, we returned to Chaffin's on the 11th, and the next day watched the smoke rising over the field of battle on the south side of the James when Wise's men struck the enemy under Butler not far from Drewry's Bluff. For nearly two weeks we remained stationary, ready to aid our friends on the south side of the river, or to join the Army of Northern Virginia in its resistance to Grant's powerful army on the North Anna.

On the 22nd of May we left Chaffin's for the last time and marched to Anderson's Crossing, where Pickett's division was again united, and became once more an active arm of that grand army, whose fame, so honestly won, has been the admiration of the world.

On the 24th of May the division prepared to meet the enemy between the Virginia Central railroad and the North

Anna river, but they came not. Early in the morning of the 27th (before day) our regiment was put in motion, and that evening we found ourselves in the trenches facing the enemy, who was expected to attack us. Again on the 28th we looked for an attack, but no enemy approached the works where we were. Late in the evening of that day the writer was detailed for outpost duty with instructions to select from the regiment two of the best men, to be stationed at a very important angle. Lon Lane and Joe Points, both of Company A (than whom better soldiers nor braver spirits ever shouldered a musket) were selected. The detail stepped over the breastworks just about dark, and were stationed as instructed. To the important angle the writer with Lane and Points were guided in the dark, and there spent one of the longest (seemingly) nights of the war. We had to lie prostrate all night, peeping over a small mound of dirt, expecting every minute to hear and see the approaching enemy. The next morning we returned to the breastworks, but before eating or sleeping, the line was extended to the right, and when we did halt we momentarily expected an attack and could not sleep. This was the time when Grant, becoming satisfied that he could not break through Lee's line, had hurried to his left, expecting to find an easy and short road to Richmond from the vicinity of Cold Harbor. Lee extended his right so rapidly that on every occasion when our line was approached, the enemy found the boys in gray disputing his right to pass. Excuse me. I am not writing history, but personal reminiscences.

On the evening of June the first heavy firing on the right was heard. For awhile we moved leisurely to the right along the breastworks. Soon, however, we left the breastworks and double-quicked to the right, through a wooded country, up a branch, and about dark took position on a hill in a broomsedge field dotted over with old-field pines. Here we were shelled for about an hour with no opportunity to return the punishment in kind. An energetic member of Company A used his bayonet so industriously that he completed a snug riflepit just as we were ordered forward and took possession of some old works that doubtless saw service in 1862. Here we spent the night. On June 2d we marched forward and took position on a hill with woods in front and cleared land in the rear. The day was with us a quiet one, but occasionally the roaring cannon reminded us of the enemy's proximity.

About dark I spread my oil-cloth and was happy in anticipation of a night's sleep which I so much needed. Scarcely had I become oblivious to surroundings, however, before the voice of J. D. McIntire, acting Adjutant, was heard, calling my name. "You are detailed for outpost duty," came in response to my "Here I am." Officers were scarce and my turn had come even before I had caught up in sleep. I was furnished with a guide and instructed to report to Major Boyd—one of those hard fighters of Company G from Nelson county. Not a star was to be seen. Now and then it sprinkled rain. My instructions were —"Speak seldom and then in a whisper—listen attentively and report anything you hear. Be prudent, the enemy's pickets are within thirty paces." I knew not where I was nor whom I commanded. I was told "six posts are on your line" and supposed the men were of the Nineteenth. Passing from one soldier to the other I found them alert and safely located each behind a big tree. I accidentally broke a twig which drew a shot from the enemy without harm to any one.

About midnight I heard distinctly the enemy at work. They seemed to be driving piles into the ground with muffled mauls. They were evidently planting artillery. Upon reporting this to Major Boyd I was instructed to go to the rear and make a report to General Hoke. Turning my back upon the picket line I moved cautiously rearward through the woods, and had not gone far before I was knee-deep in swamp mud. A little further and into a small stream I plunged, from which I was unable to climb except in the direction from which I came. I concluded to go down the branch and to my dismay found myself stumbling over the bodies of dead men whom I ascertained, by feeling, to be United States soldiers. They were killed the day before in a skirmish, and being between the lines had not received proper attention. Wandering further down the branch after making several unsuccessful attempts to climb the high bank on the other side, I became conscious of the presence of some one else. Friend or foe, I knew not. Whether or not the branch ran into the enemy's line I could not tell. I whispered "Who are you?" and my name was called in a whisper by Lieutenant Jesse Richeson of Amherst county, who, like myself, was on outpost that dark dismal night.

Richeson furnished me with a guide, and I made my report to General Hoke, from whose headquarters I sought those of the Nineteenth where, casting myself upon the damp leaves about two a.m., I slept soundly until called upon to take my place in the beginning of that terrible third day of June, 1864.

The Battle Of
Cold Harbor

Early in the morning of June the third, 1864, the Nine-teenth Virginia Regiment took position in the woods to act a part in the second battle of Cold Harbor. The regiment did not form a connected line of battle, but there was considerable space between the companies, thus covering nearly twice the usual front in battle. In this arrangement Company K, commanded by Lieutenant Robertson, was thrown forward of the other companies, and being near the centre of the regimental line was most exposed. The troops in the woods were not protected by earthworks. In fact, there seemed to be a gap in the general line of earthworks at this point, and we had been selected to prevent the passage of the gap by the enemy. We had not long to wait before the enemy opened upon us from every tree and log in our front, and by the roar of musketry off to our left, we knew the enemy was charging our lines. A lull on the left was followed by heavy firing in that direction, as column after column was hurled back from our works, leaving the ground blue with the dead and dying. In our immediate front, however, the fight was much of a bushwhacking affair on both sides.

Late in the action I received an order to hasten to Company K and take command, as all the officers of that company had been killed. Captain Culin of Company A had been wounded, and in obeying the order I left the company in command of Sergeant Perley. I did not reach Company K until just as the enemy withdrew, but in time to see the disaster that had overtaken that band of stern fighters. The fight had lasted about sixty minutes, and in that time the best and bravest again had fallen. Sergeant-Major Luther Wolfe was killed; Lieutenant Evans of Company C and Lieutenant Robertson of Company K were killed; but the greatest loss to the regiment was James G. Woodson of Company K, who, as senior captain, was in command of the regiment.

Captain Woodson was a modest, quiet Christian gentleman, with a high sense of honor, and a great regard for duty. No ordeal however trying, no service however irksome, would he hesitate to dare and do if in the line of duty. He was incapacitated for active duty by the loss of a toe at Gettysburg, which made walking painful; and the day he was killed was further incapacitated by illness. The surgeon and personal friends urged him not to go into the battle, but he knew the Colonel was absent, and the command devolved upon him, and go he would. The list of casualties as published in the *Examiner* the next day mentioned "Capt. J. G. Woodson acting major killed." Scarcely had the morning papers containing the list reached the regiment on the 5th, when could be seen squads of men throughout the regiment, regardless of company, discussing the list of casualties. Towards noon an indignation meeting was held, and in the *Enquirer* of the 6th or 7th the following card appeared as a result thereof:

"In justice to the memory of Capt. James G. Woodson of Company K, Nineteenth Virginia Regiment, we state, that when killed on the 3d instant he was in command of the regiment.

(Signed)

"R. J. Harland, Capt. Company D.

"Chas. S. Irving, Capt. Company C.

"W. N. Wood, Lieut., Company A."

This plain statement of facts gave rise to some hard feelings, and was the cause of trouble to the one whose name was last among the signers of the card, he avowing its authorship to the Colonel.

General Grant seems to have become satisfied of his inability to whip the army of Northern Virginia, and an idea of strategy seems to have entered his brain. He even dared an effort to outgeneral the matchless Lee. In this, his failure equalled that of his fighting, for when he crossed to the south side of the James and advanced towards the railroad between Richmond and Petersburg, he found Pickett's division in his front.

Marching leisurely along the pike between the two cities mentioned above, on the 17th of June we arrived at a point nearly opposite Chester on the railroad (the pike is east of the railroad) when a halt was made. One single musket shot had just been heard in front of us. The writer was addressed as follows: "Lieutenant, deploy your company as skirmishers and advance." Captain Culin had drilled the company thoroughly as skirmishers. We quickly deployed, and rapidly advanced for several hundred yards without meeting any opposition. I sent a messenger to the Colonel asking for further instructions, but received no reply save in the shape of Company C, Captain Charles Irving commanding, who deployed his company on the left of Company A. We continued the advance and soon came to a small field (we had been in the woods all the time) near the center of which stood an old barn that rested on pillars about two feet high. Stooping, we plainly saw blue pants under the barn and knew we had found what we were looking for. We advanced the right and left of our line some distance, and with a yell the center rushed, at a double quick, upon the barn, but before we reached it, the blue pants were flying into the woods beyond the field.

Upon a hurried consultation, it was agreed to continue the advance until we met with some formidable obstacle. We expected the brigade was following us, but it turned out that at least a mile lay between us. We now moved cautiously and with less celerity, but continued to go forward. We soon emerged into a large opening, and immediately in front was a line of formidable-looking earthworks. Another hasty consultation. Must we advance upon the works? We had in all about forty muskets, but every musket was in the hands of a soldier, "Boys, yell like demons. Forward! double quick!" and away we went, making noise enough for a brigade, and fortunately, kicking up so much dust that the enemy doubtless thought it prudent to leave the works before our arrival, and thus we regained the earthworks on the Howlett line that had been vacated by Beauregard's troops when hurried to the defense of Petersburg.

Here we concluded to halt until further instructed. Dispatching a messenger to the command, we deployed in order to occupy as much space as possible. It was nearly night and with no little anxiety did we watch for the coming of the brigade. Finally it was dark and no aid, or word even, had reached us. We put out videttes and began the watching of the night. Every man was a sentinel and every sentinel was a tried soldier, but here again the excellence as watchers of Lon Lane and Joe Points, suggested their use as videttes at the most exposed points. Our peril was duly appreciated by every man present, and no hint even was necessary to secure watchfulness. The writer walked from one end of our line to the other several times that night, and listened intently for aid from the rear, and most fearfully for the enemy's tread in front. Neither came, but finally a dawn in the east gave promise of the end of the night. Videttes were called in, and we concluded to sleep by detail, with the musket by each sleeper and cartridge-box not removed, but our plans were rendered null by the arrival of the brigade about sun up. The line was extended and strengthened, and these trenches became our abiding place for many months.

CHAPTER XV

The Last Of The
Nineteenth

Dig a ditch two and a half feet deep, five or six feet wide, and heap up the dirt on the side toward the enemy, and you will have trenches for infantry. Earthworks for artillery are more scientifically built—more dirt and more trench. The approach to Richmond was cut off by trenches guarded largely by infantry and had the appearance of a long dirt fence with men peeping over at every yard. In front of the trenches—toward the enemy—were small ditches at intervals of thirty to one hundred and fifty feet, called rifle-pits, used by sentinels at night, and sometimes in the day, to give the alarm should the enemy advance. Sometimes it so happened that the trenches of the enemy were so near that rifle-pits were not admissible. At different points on the line old-field pines, or original woods or cliffs of rocks, intervened between the trenches and offered excellent opportunities for stealthy advances and unwelcome surprises, as well as giving sometimes favorable chances for sly meetings of opposing pickets or sentries where usually tobacco was traded for coffee, or papers exchanged. We built huts just back of the trenches or erected sheds, or pitched an old tent, and in some instances furrowed in the ground and made "bomb-proofs" in order to be really comfortable.

As stated in my last communication, we took possession of the trenches on the Howlett line, extending from the James to the Appomattox in mid-summer, and had not much need of houses or tents, but as the winter approached each mess became industriously engaged in making preparations for long nights and cold days, when life in the trenches assumed its brightest and most cheerful aspect. In our division we had a Masonic lodge with Adjutant C. C. Wertenbaker as master. Many bright Masons resulted from this effort, notably W. T. Rea, one of the brightest in the State today. We had chapels where protracted services were held by ministers of different denominations, where many a soldier was born into the king-dom of Christ. We had debating societies and discussed such questions as Decatur's motto—"My country; may she be always right, but right or wrong, my country." We had chess clubs, where several men learned to play a good game of chess while blindfolded. We had several newspaper correspondents, who furnished weekly communications to various papers. We had reading clubs, at which profound histories, sublime poems, as well as light literature, were enjoyed. Nearly every one played checkers, and not a few "threw the papers" as card-playing was called. I have now in possession a set of chess-men made on the Howlett line, which saw service then, and afterwards served me well in the old Capitol and on Johnson's Island, of which more in due time. Of course, we had to take our turn at duty in the trenches and in the rifle-pits. Some would get sick and be sent to Chester; some would secure leave of absence and visit Richmond, and some few would secure furloughs and make a visit home.

We lived on fairly good terms with our neighbors across the way, and occasionally enlivened things by a dash at their lines to ascertain their strength. Now and then a prisoner was wanted—just to see, I suppose, what command was in front of us—and a resort to strategy, usually supplied the want.

I might mention our athletic sports—wrestling, running, jumping, boxing, etc., all of which were keenly relished by these grown-up boys. Then, I could write pages upon the sentimental side of the life in trenches. There was much visiting and several marriages. During our nine months stay in the trenches, rations were scarce, very scarce, and oh! the delights of a box from home!

The summer vanished. The fall season passed by. The winter had well nigh departed when, after stretching our line to the right until there was scarcely a skirmish line left to defend the works, we were ordered late in March, 1865, to get ready to leave the the trenches. We had made a flying trip up the Southside railroad and returned, and then crossed the James and returned. On the morning of the 31st of March our brigade (Hunton's) was near Hatcher's run. The other brigades of the division had been hurried off elsewhere to meet the advancing foe. We were not lonely, however, for we saw the manly form of R. E. Lee sitting on "Traveller" near where we halted on the roadside. In a few minutes a courier rode up and stopped a minute or two at the head of our regiment. "Boys! prepare for action!" was quietly spoken by some one, and in a few minutes a line of battle was formed. The word "Forward!" was distinctly heard, and we moved forward in battle array. Entering a body of second growth pines we became conscious of the "zip! zip!" of the minnie-ball from the concealed foe in the pines. Orders came—"Forward at a double quick!" and soon we were chasing the blue coats through the pines with General Lee on "Traveller" in our midst. "Don't go with us General, but watch us," came from the line, and "Traveller" halted with his master, while we bounded forward with renewed energy. About this time I was informed that Captain Culin was wounded and the command of the company devolved upon me. We were halted very soon —just as an entrenched line of the enemy appeared in front. We had run them into their breastworks, and halted just in time to escape a seeming trap, for bullets had begun to come from front and left. Protecting ourselves behind the pines, we went to work with our accustomed earnestness. I had secured a musket, returned my army pistol to the holster, and taken position behind a small pine, where I watched the line and used the musket to the best advantage. I had stepped back from the pine in order to reload and with body turned to the left was sending a ball home, when a seeming blow on the back of the neck accompanied by a burning sensation, caused me to quickly pass my hand to the injured part, and found myself bleeding profusely. Dropping my musket I hurried to the rear, and approached Dr. Taylor with the question: "Am I hurt much?" He examined the wound, dressed it and then said: "One thirty-second of an inch nearer and you would not have known what struck you." In thirty minutes I returned to duty with a bandaged neck and the only war scar that has lasted to the present day.

We slowly fell back from our advanced position, remaining in line of battle. That night we began the movement that was a march without progress, a stopping without a halt. Our brigade was not at Five Forks with the remainder of the division, consequently did not share *the defeat of the war* by Pickett's division, and when joined by the remnant of that disaster we could no more be called a division. I have no means of ascertaining our speed in this retreat, but I am sure an hour's time was frequently consumed in making a mile. What was the matter? Simply the muddy roads and half-fed horses. It was impossible to move the wagon trains rapidly. I was in command of Company A, and made numerous efforts to secure rations for the company, but it was impossible. Without bread, without rest, without sleep, we were in no mood to learn that Richmond was in the hands of the enemy. Our faith in R. E. Lee never faltered, and though we felt that every step was one from home, to we knew not where, we chewed our grains of unparched corn and kept our powder dry.

By the 5th of April many of the company were suffering so much from hunger, that I detailed two men to go in search of something to eat. They were "cut off" and never returned to the command. They could not get back. On the 6th of April we halted on a hill overlooking what I have always thought was Sailor's creek. "Now, boys, make a fire and parch some corn." The fire was made and the frying pan of corn was placed thereon, but ere a single grain had browned, the message came, "Lieutenant! take your company and cross the creek and clear the road and pines in front. The command will follow you." Hurriedly dividing the warmed corn, and pouring it into empty haver-sacks, the Old Monticello Guard, Company A, Nineteenth Virginia Infantry, was formed for the last time, and marched down the hill, across the creek and deployed in the pines as skirmishers. We drove the enemy, recaptured a few pieces of artillery and rallied on the center. The command followed us, and we took our position at the head of the regiment. We followed the road up the hill through the woods, and halted in the field on the road-side.

Behind us was a small field of cleared land that had not been cultivated for years. In front of us was cleared land that had been recently cultivated, and away over in front were hills of cleared land upon which horsemen without number seemed to be gathering. How numerous were the foe and how rapidly those hills were covered! Arranging fence rails in front of us, and taking advantage of any unevenness in the ground, we made ready to receive our visitors. I had just said to Dick McMullen, "Be sure not to fire until they reach that mullein stalk," when a commotion in the rear of our line caused me to look behind us, and to my dismay, my eyes rested upon the largest line of cavalry I had ever seen. There seemed to be no end to the line. There they stood in double ranks within forty feet of us. They were well mounted and admirably armed. How they got there in our immediate rear I know not, and from what direction they came I have never learned. The fact is, they were there in overpowering numbers, with pistol or gun ready to do damage upon the least show of resistance. Major Boyd, commanding our regiment, quickly said: "We are prisoners," and that was the end of the Nineteenth Virginia Infantry as a body of armed soldiers.

CHAPTER XVI

Life In Prison

I was taken to Washington, and lodged in the Old Capitol Prison. I was there when Lincoln was assassinated; the mob on the streets was so great, it was necessary to double the guards around the prison.

My few days there were not uncomfortable, except from the warm weather. We were fed on pork and beans and hard tack. We were then taken to Johnson's Island, in Lake Erie. As the war was over, discipline was relaxed, and "we boys" had very good times. All who were so fortunate as to have friends to send them greenbacks were granted permission to buy what they wanted from the sutler, and our fare was thereby improved.

Chess was our favorite amusement. As the prisoners were released alphabetically, my name was among the last, and I was not released till June, 1865. Most of the other men were gone, transportation was given us, but no rations, and I was without money, except Confederate notes.

The men had left a number of blankets in the prison, and I bargained with one of the sentinels to throw some up to him, on the wall, when the officer on duty had passed to the other side of the yard. I succeeded in selling four to him, for which he paid me fifty cents each. When I left, I filled my knapsack with the old clothes left by the men, and rolled up some Federal blankets in my Confederate one.

When I reached Milwaukee, I stood on the street corner, opened my knapsack, and sold most of the contents to passersby for seven dollars. I gave one suit of clothes to an Irishman, who had no money to pay for them.

I travelled, via Baltimore to Richmond, thence to Charlottesville, and walked to my father's home near there, where I was glad to don some clean citizen's clothes, that my mother had kept for me through the war, and to eat a good dinner.

Though greatly crushed by the final outcome of our struggle, I felt proud that I had been permitted to do my part, and even to suffer for the cause I loved. Some comfort was derived from the contemplation that there would be no more blood shed; but peace, with all it meant to a tired soldier, was at hand.

CHAPTER XVII

After Thirty-Seven Years

It was recently my good fortune to be a partaker of old Virginia hospitality in the famous town of Warrenton, Virginia, for several days.

I visited the beautiful cemetery where lie buried six hundred Confederate soldiers to whose memory an imposing monument has been erected by the ladies of the town. I lingered at the grave of Captain John Marr, the first man killed in battle in the war between the States. Had a long talk with General Eppa Hunton, in which battles were fought again and episodes recalled that turned the memory back to other days and other scenes. Thus catching afresh the inspiration of sixty-one and five, I was glad to hear from mine hostess— "We will have a picnic on the battlefield of Manassas tomorrow." The tomorrow came. Leaving Warrenton at an early hour behind a pair of good trotters, we took the pike and

77

went direct to the Stone bridge over the Bull Run, passing Gainsville, Groveton and other places of interest. The bridge is unchanged, but the bottom land southeast of it is now covered with trees—many of them fifty feet high—grown since sixty-one. Cross roads and fences have been changed, and lands are now in cultivation that were in woods then, and *vice versa.*

Retracing our way along the pike, we turned in at the Robinson house, and the writer mounted the fence and gazed over the land. I looked westward over the valley to the hills beyond—now so peaceful and quiet, then so full of life and activity. Returning to the pike and moving southward we soon came to the road that branched off to the Henry house. As we approached this noted spot there was a profound stillness; save two calves in the shade, not a sign of life in sight, no groans, no shrieks, no wild rushing of horses; no rattle of musketry; no booming of cannon. How changed the scene on that plateau since that hot Sunday—July 21, 1861.

The old Henry house has been torn down and a new one built on the same site. I stood for a while and mused; within a stone's throw was the heaviest fighting. Just over the fence the name of Stonewall was given Jackson. There fell Bee, and not far off fell Bartow. How thickly lay the dead and wounded as the sun sunk in the west on that eventful 21st of July.

We next visited the Conrad house and there spread our lunch on the grass in the shade and had a picnic on the battle-field of First Manassas. Here we found a well of excellent water—an article that was not found by many on that hot Sunday. This Conrad house is often spoken of as the Chinn house by mistake. It was in the rear of this house and very near it, that nine companies of the Nineteenth Virginia Regiment formed a line of battle near the close of the fight, thirty-eight years ago, and watched the shells from Kemper's battery play upon the rapidly retreating foe, as they rushed up the hill in wild confusion beyond the Stone bridge.

We turned from the field of First Manassas to visit the scenes of the last days of August, eighteen hundred and sixty-two. A gentle trot of about a mile brought us to the Chinn house, the center of interest to the Nineteenth Virginia Regiment, for it was near this house that Hunton's brigade of which the Nineteenth was a part, engaged the enemy on the last day of the second Manassas fight—August 30th, eighteen hundred and sixty-two, aiding in driving them pell-mell from the hotly contested field. The writer walked over a portion of the field and could almost tell the spot where comrades fell. Just there R. C. Vandegrift received a wound, and not far off W. A. Johnson and others fell to rise no more. A little further up the bottom Captain H. Clay Michie of the Fifty-Sixth received a wound. That hill, crowned with the enemy's artillery then, was the scene of Colonel Skinner's daring dash with his long sabre, which he so efficiently used as Kemper's brigade charged the guns. That other hill is where John LeTellier turned the enemy's guns upon the retreating column—quickening their steps toward Yankeedom, and between the two hills floated the lone star of Texas as Hood's men fearlessly struggled with a mass of blue coats.

The hills do not look so high nor steep now as then, but distances seem greater.

We visited Groveton, another place of interest. It was near Groveton that Jackson formed his line of battle in the unfinished railroad, and repelled the violent attacks of Pope's heavy columns time and again before Longstreet reached the field of action. Thus ended the most pleasant day the writer ever spent on a battlefield.

THE APPENDIX

APPENDIX I

TWO WAR-TIME LETTERS OF
WILLIAM NATHANIEL WOOD

Were I at home I might be your Rival. Make hay while the sun shines. *Court Mollie*—She is a Sweet Girl.

In Camp at Centreville Aug 13/61

Dear Brother

I wrote you a few lines [several] days since stating that we had [received] marching orders . . . when we stopped. We moved only one mile and are now stationed [near] that place they call Centreville. We have had rain for three days and it has [been very uncomfortable. I stood] guard one dark night during [that heavy downpour.] I got somewhat wet but with a soldiers heroism I took it patiently. Today is my *wash day* but as the sun is hid behind the clouds I have concluded to postpone that job. It is quite cool here this morning and [we find the] Yankee overcoats quite serviceable and I have mine . . . with buttons on which is stamped the New York coat of arms. If the Yankees had [not brought] us these useful articles I am thinking that we might have suffered slightly. The Chance for a fight with us Seems to be quite a poor one, but I Suppose old Beauregard knows what is what and we therefore take our ease, but Should you hear of a fight down here you can come down to See *whether anybody is hurt or not.* I wish we could get a chance and thrash the Scamps into an acknowledgement of our independence So we could return to our homes by the first of December but Since we cannot have it as we would like we must take it as it is.

You may have my buckskin over gaiters made as soon as

possible, have them made to fit you, let them extend up to the knee and fit the calf well, Smaller in the Ankle extending over the Shoe some distance with Straps running under the foot or Shoe, let there be four small Buckles to fasten it, one Buckle at top one buckle at the bottom at ankle and the other two at equal distances one will be at the *Calf.* You can have them made so the Buckles will be on the *Out* Side of the leg, have small straps to which the buckles will fasten so that I can loosen them easy. I can't tell you who will make them, but Should you find any difficulty about them make a pair [of] Cloth ones, heavy *Duck* either Cotton or Linen makes very good ones, I never saw a pair of *Buck* ones but imagined that it would make a good pair. If you cant get them made, look in the room that Dick Flannagan and I occupied and you will find a pair of Short ones belonging to me which you can Send by someone passing. Some Persons have patterns for them but I do not recollect of any one now except Miss Kate Stockton who I Suppose Since being married never thinks of *Legings* any more, However do the best you can & you will please me. The Buckskin may be too heavy I am afraid it is, you can be judge of that.

Tell Pennie to look in the *Safe* Cash Drawer and he will find a little ticket against the taylor, Mr. Harris, which you can have worked out and charge to me, There is a Small Credit on the Ticket which is correct. Ask Mr. Crigler to make a statement of the day I left Town which was 18th July and put it in the Safe. I intend to say the day I left his Service which was the day above named and should I never come home you can settle up my little affairs. You know where my . . . [one word illegible] is. You will Remember that I have a Bond due me which can be found in a little Bag in my Trunk—There is an open a/c between Mr. Foster and myself but say nothing about that as he owes me the same amount that I owe him. he has it charged against me but I have nothing to Show against him. You can remember that and Should I fall on the field you then can have it Settled. I owe some debts but you can easily pay them with my funds but let them *all* be as they are as long as I remain a *living* Soldier as I have bright hopes of surviving this war, Remembering at the same time that I stand a good chance to fall victim to the Enemie's balls or else dread disease may lay its violent hand upon my youthful form & hurry me from the Scenes of earthly action I have no other instructions to give.

Send me nothing more to eat until I Send you word for my box has not given out yet, & the camp eatables are not so bad. We have Flour in abundance, coffee & Sugar Sufficient and beef to such an extent that it becomes a nuisance. Ham is plentiful in *our* tent, Butter too is at our command, molasses now & then finds its way to the tent which I am so fortunate as to be a member of, In fact our tent's inhabitants live like fighting chickens. We have a Servant to cook for us, plenty Tobacco to smoke and truly we are quite a contented set of *Boys.*

Tell Spencer more generally known as "Bumshell" that my shoes haven't been blacked since *he* blacked them. Tell them at home how well I am pleased and ask them not to be uneasy about me. Write to Mildred often and keep her informed as to my proceedings. I will try and write her soon but I have so many *Ladies* to write to that I am kept tolerably busy. I drill twice per day once in Company drill and once in Battallion drill besides dress parade which I will attend as soon as I get my uniform which will be in a few days. I spend a good portion of my time in reading and every four or five days I am on duty for twenty four hours—standing as Sentinel eight hours out of the twenty four.

I will write to *your affiancee* in a few days if not this evening. I Suppose the Cadets have long since sunk into oblivion. You I would hope are very punctual in going to

Sunday School & Church. I am glad to know that the Regiment or at least our Company attribute our safety during the fight of July 21st to the prayers of God's people of Charlottesville. May they take fresh Courage, May their Faith be Strengthened and may their prayers with renewed brightness ascend to that God who has promised to hear His people when they call upon His holy name. Surely we need your prayers. Christians should be zealous in our cause, pray for Success, pray for our Salvation, pray for a speedy honorable peace, Recognise God as the giver of every blessing. Remember that it is not all of life to live nor all of death to death to die. In Heaven there is no war, May God bless you My Dear Brother and all our Friends & Relatives. Give my Love to all my Friends.

Your affectionate Bro

Nat

Look in my trunk at home and Send me a fine comb also Send me a pocket comb that you will find in my jacket pocket in the trunk at Mr. Flannagan
Give my Love to all Friends

Camp Near Culpepper C. H.
November 4th 1862

Dear Ones at home

I have realised my fond expectation in leaving the Valley and pitching our bush huts near the Rail Road Here we are in Culpepper County about two miles from the C. H. I have made an application for twenty four hours leave of absence and it has just returned "disapproved" by the Major General Of course they have good reasons for not allowing me to visit home but I do think a little hard of them, I am Sadly in need of many articles of clotheing and Since I can't visit you to get them, I must ask you to put yourselves to the trouble of getting the following articles for me, One pair Shoes No. 7; let them be good Strong ones, I want two (2) cotton or calico Shirts, I don't care what the Shirts are made of, and two (2) pair Socks; Send to Mr. R K Flannagan and he will give you my trunk, and my uniform coat if he has had it cleaned; Mr. Flannagan will also give you two hundred (200) Dollars that I Sent him recently. You will find one over Shirt, one linen Shirt and two pairs Drawers in the trunk also a pair *blue* pants as well as many other articles of camp use, Take care of every thing in the trunk and Send me only the Shirts, drawers, and the blue pants, The trunk does not belong to me and I don't know what you can get to Send my Clothes in; I would like to have a Smaller trunk but that you can't find anywhere; I think it would be advisable to make a Small box, provided you can't get a hand trunk, or a large Size Carpet bag would answer every purpose. I will write to Mr. Flannagan and ask him to get one for me it may be that Some kind friend will let him have one when he tells them it is for me, when you have gotten the above mentioned things pack them up with a towel or two and Some *Soap* and send them to Mr. Flannagan and he will Send them to me, and when you make me the pair pants I wrote for in my last letter, you can Send them in the Same way. I fear that we are going to South Carolina or Somewhere "way down in Dixie" and I would like to be a decent man again, the fact is, I have not changed Socks for two months and I am compelled to borrow Shirts & Drawers to get mine washed. I have lost so much clothing that I Sometimes think of being a negro at once and be done with it, but I think I have gotten a Sure way of carrying my clothes in the future provided I don't have a too large trunk; I have marched, fought, Slept and eat like Someone destitute of all traits of Civilization, but it was because great demands were made upon us, and we had to Stand up to the Rack or be whipped by the cowardly Yankees. I am still the Same old Nat, and with the help of God I will

Stand by my boys until the last gun is fired or else upon the battle field my lifeless body Shall lay. I have been Shamefully forsaken by my Company officers, but Still I have in the Company men who will Stand by me as long as life last; I am an advocate of Peace but before I will Submit to the rule of Abraham Lincoln I will Spend my life in Camp with all its hardships & privations, I always manage to live a little better than my neighbors and if it were not flattering myself I would Say that I am respected by my fellow officers as highly as any one in the Regiment. Jim Birkhead will be court martialed and will have to pay for the Gun he lost when he so Shamefully ran home; I frequently ride when on marches, and in fact I have not much hardships to undergo after all; I certainly do pity the privates but after all they are as happy as a lord

I want to hire a negro boy or man, I will give fifteen dollars a month for one to wait on me, Can I get one from any body in your neighborhood. If one can be had hire him for me, let his Master understand that I will pay for him monthly or quarterly and Send him to Mr Flannagan with the clothes. The negro that I had went home and has not returned. I Suppose his master kept him for his own use in the Camp; Mr. Burnley proberbly could lend some light on this Subject. Negroes are perfectly Safe in camp, they get a plenty to eat and can Stay in a wagon or tent, if Sick I will Send him home where he can be attended to, and when a fight comes off, he will be out of danger with my baggage. If a negro can be had get one for me. Benjamen is well and though in need of Some things I am very much in hopes that he will get home before he Suffers for them. I never hear from Lewellen now, I imagine that he is all right. Don't be Surprised if I don't See you before next January for I will not go home until I can do it with a clear conscience and in an honorable manner, Allow yourselves to Suffer no uneasiness about me, I am in the hands of my Creator and His ways are good, His arm is round about me in him do I trust, and I know that no one need fear when He is his friend. I am beloved ones affectionately your Son &c

Nat.

In the trunk at Mr F. you will find Lizzies picture. Keep it. You will find Some things that belong to other boys. Keep them until you hear from me again.

APPENDIX II

Petition, March 27, 1863, by members of Company "A," Nineteenth Virginia Regiment for promotion of W. N. Wood to first lieutenant, and indorsement of the acting regimental commander, John T. Ellis. Courtesy Alderman Library, University of Virginia

THE PETITION

Camp 19th Va. Regt. Near Greenville, N.C.

We the undersigned members of Co. "A" 19th Va. Regt. respectfully petition that Lt. W. N. Wood, Jr 2nd Lieut. be promoted to fill the vacancy occasioned by the resignation of 1st Lieut. Henry F. Dade. We ask for the appointment through justice to Lieut. Wood whose meritorious conduct, close attendance on the Company and whose gallantry entitles him to our warmest consideration. We earnestly request that our Authorities will make the promotion asked for

Respectfully

C. H. Wingfield, O.S. Co. "A"	R. L. McMullen
Jno. C. Culin, Capt.	Chas. H. Harrison
Joseph F. Burkhead*	W. H. Brown
N. F. Burkhead	G. A. Gulley
W. W. Maury	Willis A. Herrin
J. D. Points	W. M. Dudley
W. W. Webb	James H. Dudley
A. J. Brown	Thos. J. Mooney
J. G. Burkhead	W. C. Webb
G. N. Harlow	Lorenzo Lane
J. R. Buck	J. A. Bowen
Jno. N. Pearce	W. J. Cloar

*Editor's note: The three men of this name who served in Company "A" appear in the company records as "Burkhead," "Birkhead" and "Birckhead." I have not been able to ascertain the correct spelling.

90

THE INDORSEMENT

Hq. 19 Va. Rgt.
March 27, 1863

The commanding officer feels every desire to meet the wishes of the petitioners but does not feel authorized to make appointments of officers as he is the Junior officer and his Senior Colonel Gantt will return in a few days.

John T. Ellis
Lt. Col. Comdg.

APPENDIX III

ROLL OF COMPANY "A" NINETEENTH VIRGINIA REGIMENT

Courtesy Alderman Library, University of Virginia

ROLL OF MONTICELLO GUARD, CO. "A" 19 VIRGA. AT CENTREVILLE

Capt. Wm. B. Mallory	Detailed as Post Com., May, 1862
1st. Lt. C. C. Wertenbaker	Transf. to Staff, May, 1862
2nd. Lt. J. N. C. Stockton	Transf. to Brigade Adjt., May '62
3rd. Lt. J. C. Culin	Elected Capt. May 1862
1st. Sgt. H. F. Dade	Elected 1st Lieut. May 1862
2nd. Sgt. R. W. Bailey	Elected 2nd Lieut. May 1862
3rd. Sgt. W. B. LeTellier	Transf. to Co. "E"
4th Sgt. T. J. Wingfield	
5th Sgt. A. H. Hoffman	Killed at Williamsburg
QM Dr. R. G. Bailey	
1 Corpl. C. H. Wingfield	
2 Corpl. James Perley	
3 Corpl. Geo. A. Gulley	
4 Corpl. Chas. Lightbaker	Transferred
Private John A. Allen	Killed at Williamsburg
Bailey, G. W.	
Buck, J. R.	Captured at Gettysburg
Bacon, W. O.	
Bacon, D. W.	

Brown, W. A.

Brown, Jas. J.

Bowman, Jos. H. Discharged Dec. 1861

Birckhead, Jos. F.

Batchellor, J. C. Transferred

Collier, J. W. H.

Collier, H. H.

*Collier, Jas. Killed at Seven Pines

Culin, Wm.

Culin, Geo. W.

Cloar, Jno. W. Discharged Sept. 1861

Cloar, W. J.

Cloar, Jas. L.

Clark, W. D.

Christian, Jno. J. Killed at Boonesborough

Degan, Henry Discharged Sept. 1862

Dodd, Jno. B.

Dobbins, R. L.

Durrett, Jno. D.

Foster, W. R.

Fuller, Jos.

Franks, Wm. B. Discharged July 1862

Frease, H. P.

Goolsby, J. M.

Gibson, Jos.

*Jas. Collier was killed at Seven Pines while acting as a temporary substitute for H. H. Collier. He was a mere lad, and was never regularly enlisted.

Goodwin, Louis C.	Discharged June 1862
Harman, Chas. H.	Transferred
Hudson, Andrew	Transferred
Houchens, J. W.	Captured at Gettysburg
Houchens, Thos. M.	
Hill, J. W. (3rd Lieut. Aug. '63)	Killed at Gettysburg
Johnson, Geo. T.	Captured at Gettysburg
Johnson, W. A.	Killed at 2nd Manassas
Jones, L. S.	Killed at Gettysburg
Jones, Jas. R.	Killed at Seven Pines
Jones, Wm. T.	Wounded & captured at Williamsburg
Kidd, Wm. P.	Killed at Seven Pines
Kenny, Chas.	
Kelley, Saml. A.	
Liady, A. G.	Discharged July 1862
Lorsch, H. L.	Discharged April 1864
Lee, Jno. W.	
Mallory, Jos. E.	2nd Lieut. May 1862
Mallory, Geo. J.	Discharged January 1862
McMullen, R. L.	
McMullen, Jno. W.	
McMullen, Geo. A.	Died in Hospital
Moran, Geo. M.	Discharged Aug. 1862
McKenna, John	Discharged July 1862
Maury, Wirt W.	Discharged April 1864
Mooney, T. J.	

O'Toole, Pat.	Discharged June 1862
Points, Polk	Killed at Gettysburg
Perley, Wm. E.	
Pearce, Jno. N.	
Pearce, Marion L.	Killed at Seven Pines
Payne, Wm. C.	Discharged June 1862
Points, Jos. D.	
Quicke, Jas. M.	
Randolph, Thos. J.	Killed at Boonesborough
Rumbaugh, Jacob	
Seayden, Jos. W.	
Seargeant, N. R.	
Shannon, Patrick	Transferred
Sales, Mat G.	Died in Hospital
Snead, Gid S.	Transferred
Troeter, Louis C.	
Vaughn, W. H.	
Vandegrift, C. W.	Wounded & captured at Williamsburg
Vandegrift, R. C.	Transferred
Wertenbaker, T. G.	Died in Hospital (2)
Wingfield, R. F.	
Wingfield, T. F.	
Wingfield, M. W.	
Wingfield, A. C.	Discharged August 1863
Wingfield, R. L.	Discharged
Wilkins, Geo. W.	Transferred

Webb, W. W.

Webb, W. C.

Wood, W. N.   Elected 3rd Lieut. and afterwards
                                 promoted to 2nd Lieut.

Williams, T. J.   Transferred

JOINED MAY 1ST, 1862

Bowen, Jno. A.   Missing at Gettysburg

Brown, A. J.

Birckhead, Jas. F.

Birckhead, N. F.

Copeland, N. F.

Lane, Lorenzo

Humphreys, J. E.   Deserted

Lane, T. E.

Thomas, J. W.

ADDITIONAL NAMES ON ROLL OF MAY 1863

Brooks, A. J.

Dennis, Jno. M.

Dudley, Jas.   Missing at Gettysburg

Dudley, Wm.   Missing at Gettysburg

Herron, W. A.

Harlow, G. N.

Harrison, C. H.

Haw, Thomas   D

Leaky, Danl.   D

Wingfield, T. F.   Killed at Fraziers Farm

ON ROLL OF OCTOBER 1863

Harlow, J. M.

Herron, J. A.

Jones, Jas. H.

Roads, C. W.   Killed at ————

ON ROLL OF APRIL 1864

Baldwin, J. W.

Clicks, Wm.   Discharged

Joseph Mooney

APPENDIX IV

DESCRIPTIVE LIST OF ENLISTED MEN IN COMPANY "A," NINETEENTH VIRGINIA REGIMENT

(Editor's Note: There is some inconsistency in the spelling of names in this and the roll in Appendix III. Since it is impossible to ascertain which copyist was right—both doubtless made errors—it was thought best to reproduce the spellings just as they appeared on the rolls.)

	Name	Rank	Age	Eyes	Hair	Complexion	Feet	Height Inches
1.	C. H. Wingfield	1st Sgt.	25	Dark	Dark	Light	5	10½
2.	James Perley	Sgt.	30	Gray	Dark	Ruddy	5	5
3.	W. W. Maury	Sgt.	44	Hazel	Sandy	Ruddy	5	6
4.	D. M. Bacon	Sgt.	23	Blue	Sandy	Ruddy	6	1
5.	Jas. R. Buck	Sgt.						
6.	Geo. T. Johnson	Corpl.						
7.	W. O. Bacon	Pvt.	21	Blue	Sandy	Florid	5	10
8.	Polk Points	Col. Corp.						
9.	Wm. H. Brown	Pvt.	32	Gray	Dark	Florid	5	2
10.	A. J. Brown	Pvt.	23	Blue	Light	Fair	5	10
11.	J. J. Brown	Pvt.	25	Blue	Light	Fair	5	11
12.	Joseph F. Birkhead	Pvt.	29	Hazel	Sandy	Red	5	7½
13.	James G. Birkhead	Pvt.	28	Gray	Dark	Light	5	10½
14.	N. S. Birkhead	Pvt.	21	Gray	Yellow	Light	5	8
15.	J. W. H. Collier	Pvt.						
16.	Wm. J. Cloar	Pvt.	24	Gray	Dark	Dark	6	1
17.	A. J. Brooks	Pvt.	21	Hazel	Black	Light	5	9½
18.	R. L. Dobbins	Pvt.	23	Gray	Black	Ruddy	5	10
19.	Jno. B. Dodd	Pvt.						
20.	John D. Durrett	Pvt.	30	Dark	Hazel	Light	6	
21.	W. M. Dudley	Pvt.						
22.	J. H. Dudley	Pvt.						
23.	James M. Dennis	Pvt.	19	Dark	Black	Light	5	6½
24.	John A. Bowen	Pvt.						
25.	John Houchens	Pvt.	24	Blue	Dark	Light	5	9

98

Courtesy Alderman Library, University of Virginia

Where Born	Occupation	When	Enlisted Where	By Whom	Period
Chville, Va.	Clerk	April 16/'61	Ch'ville	Capt. Mallory	12 mos.
Alexandria	Cabinet Maker	April 16/'61	Ch'ville	Capt. Mallory	12 mos.
Madison Co., Va.	Brick Layer	April 16/'61	Ch'ville	Capt. Mallory	12 mos.
Chville, Va.	Carpenter	April 16/'61	Ch'ville	Capt. Mallory	12 mos.
Chville, Va.	Brick Layer	April 16/'61	Ch'ville	Capt. Mallory	12 mos.
Philadelphia, Pa.	Tinner	April 16/'61	Ch'ville	Capt. Mallory	12 mos.
Buckingham	Artist	April 16/'61	Ch'ville	Capt. Mallory	12 mos.
Buckingham	Merchant	April 19/'61	Howardsville	Capt. Faulkner	12 mos.
Albemarle, Co., Va.	Farmer	April 19/'61	Howardsville	Capt. Faulkner	12 mos.
Albemarle, Co., Va.	Farmer	March 9/'62	Howardsville	Capt. Faulkner	12 mos.
Albemarle, Co., Va.	Farmer	March 8/'62	Howardsville	Capt. Duke	2 years
Albemarle, Co., Va.	Shoe Maker	April 16/'61	Howardsville	Capt. Mallory	12 mos.
Goochland Co., Va.	Boatman	August 6/'61	Fluvanna Co.	Capt. Cox	12 mos.
Albemarle Co., Va.	Shoe Maker	April 16/'61	Ch'ville	Capt. Mallory	12 mos.
Albemarle Co., Va.	Farmer	April 16/'61	Ch'ville	Capt. Mallory	12 mos.
Nelson Co., Va.	Farmer	Jan. 5/'62	Richmond	Capt. Potts	3 years
Albemarle Co., Va.	Painter	April 16/'61	Ch'ville	Capt. Mallory	

	Name	Rank	Age	Eyes	Hair	Complexion	Feet	Height Inches
26.	T. M. Houchens	Pvt.	22	Gray	Black	Light	5	9½
27.	G. W. Harlowe	Pvt.	19	Gray	Light	Light	5	5
28.	W. A. Herron	Pvt.	32	Blue	Dark	Ruddy	5	10
29.	C. H. Harrison	Pvt.	23	Blue	Light	Light	5	5
30.	Chas. Kenney	Pvt.						
31.	S. M. Kelly	Pvt.						
32.	Henry Lorch*	Pvt.	35	Gray	Black	Light	5	5
33.	Jno. W. Lee	Pvt.						
34.	Lorenzo Lane	Pvt.	19	Gray	Dark	Light	5	9
35.	R. L. McMullen	Pvt.	27	Hazel	Dark	Light	6	½
36.	T. J. Mooney	Pvt.	23	Gray	Dark	Dark	5	10
37.	Jno. N. Pearce	Pvt.	22	Hazel	Flaxen	Light	5	4½
38.	J. D. Points	Pvt.	23	Gray	Light	Light	5	7½
39.	J. E. Rumbough	Pvt.						
40.	N. R. Seargeant	Pvt.						
41.	Wm. H. Vaughan	Pvt.						
42.	R. C. Vandegrift	Pvt.	31	Blue	Light	Florid	5	11½
43.	C. W. Vandegrift	Pvt.	22	Blue	Dark	Ruddy	5	8½
44.	M. W. Wingfield	Pvt.						
45.	T. F. Wingfield	Pvt.						
46.	W. W. Webb	Pvt.	27	Hazel	Dark	Light	5	8½
47.	W. C. Webb	Pvt.	25	Blue	Flaxen	Light	5	7
48.	J. W. Thomas	Pvt.	32	Hazel	Black	Dark	6	1½
49.	C. W. Rodes	Pvt.	18	Hazel	Dark	Dark	5	8½
50.	J. M. Harlow	Pvt.	44	Gray	Dark	Dark	6	1
51.	W. A. Herron	Pvt.	42	Gray	Dark	Light	5	9
52.	James H. Jones†	Pvt.	62	Gray	Gray	Light	5	8½

*Retired
†Sub[stitute] for Howard Gray R[etire]d.

Where Born	Occupation	When	Enlisted Where	By Whom	Period
Albemarle Co., Va.	Saddler	April 16/'61	Ch'ville	Capt. Mallory	12 mos.
Fluvanna Co., Va.	Shoe Maker		Ch'ville	Capt. Boston	12 mos.
Nelson Co., Va.	Farmer	March 20/'63	Richmond	Conscript	
Baltimore, Md.	Engineer	April 12/'61	Porthmouth	Capt. Myers	12 mos.
Baden: Germany	Clerk	April 16/'61	Ch'ville	Capt. Mallory	12 mos.
Albemarle Co., Va.	Painter	March 5/'62	Ch'ville	Capt. Mallory	For war
Albemarle Co., Va.	Brick Layer	April 16/'61	Ch'ville	Capt. Mallory	12 mos.
Albemarle Co., Va.	Farmer	July 9/'61	Ch'ville	Capt. Mallory	12 mos.
Augusta Co., Va.	Tinner	July 7/'61	Ch'ville	Capt. Mallory	12 mos.
Augusta Co., Va.	Tinner	April 16/'61	Ch'ville	Capt. Mallory	12 mos.
University of Va.	Carpenter	April 16/'61	Ch'ville	Capt. Mallory	12 mos.
Albemarle Co., Va.	Carpenter	April 16/'61	Ch'ville	Capt. Mallory	12 mos.
Augusta Co., Va.	Carpenter	April 16/'61	Ch'ville	Capt. Mallory	12 mos.
Albemarle Co., Va.	Saddler	April 16/'61	Ch'ville	Capt. Mallory	12 mos.
Albemarle Co., Va.	Farmer	Sept. 3/'62	Albemarle	Conscript	
Virginia	Farmer	Aug. 17/'63	Nelson	Col. Taliafero	War
Virginia	Farmer	Sept. 5/'63	Albemarle	Lt. Mallory	War
Virginia	Farmer	Sept. 25/'63	Albemarle	Lt. Mallory	War
Penn.	Farmer	Oct. 1/'63	Camp Lee	Maj. Peyton	War

APPENDIX V

Official Reports of the Participation of the Nineteenth Virginia Regiment in the Battles of Boonsborough and Sharpsburg. These are the only reports of this regiment found in the *Official Records.*
(From: *The War of the Rebellion: A Compilation of the Official Records of the Union and Confederate Armies.* Series 1, Volume XIX, Part 1, pp. 901-902.). *Reports of Captain B. Brown, Nineteenth Virginia Infantry, of the battles of Boonsborough and Sharpsburg.*

October 15, 1862

[I have the honor to make the following] report of the battle of Slaughter's Gap, September 14:

On Sunday, September 14, the Nineteenth Virginia Regiment, numbering 150 men, after marching from Hagerstown, Md., to Boonsborough, was ordered to load and prepare for action. The sun was nearly setting behind the western hills when the regiment was formed in a line of battle on the top of a hill, with an open space in front, where the enemy lay concealed behind a stone fence, at the distance of 15 paces. A murderous fire was at once opened upon the regiment by the concealed foe, which was manfully replied to by the Nineteenth for more than an hour, when the ranks were thinned to such an extent as to prove a withdrawal absolutely necessary. One-third of the men were rendered unable to fight, and a precipitous retreat from the hill was ordered.

In this engagement Colonel J. B. Strange fell, seriously wounded, and in the retreat was left behind. His voice was heard after he had received his wound, urging his men to stand firmly, and he commanded with that coolness and daring that is found only in the truly brave. In addition to this severe loss, the regiment mourns the death of Lieutenant M. J. Shepherd, of Company B, than whom a truer patriot, a firmer officer, and a nobler youth is not found in our country's service.

The list of casualties shows the number of the brave ever to be lamented by the friends of the Nineteenth.

The command fell upon Captain John L. Cochran after the fall of Colonel Strange. Total loss, 63; names* heretofore furnished.

B. BROWN
Captain, Commanding Regiment

October 15, 1862.

[I have the honor to make the following] report of the battle of Sharpsburg, September 17:

The Nineteenth Regiment, weakened by straggling and the casualties of the 14th, was stationed on an eminent hill on the east side of Sharpsburg, with only 50 men, commanded by Lieutenant William N. Wood, acting adjutant, where they were attacked in the evening of the 17th by a large force of the enemy approaching in three directions. Under these circumstances the regiment maintained its position for two hours, when the enemy had gotten in our rear from the right, and had also passed beyond us on the left, and was pressing with vigor with ten times our number immediately in front of us. Still, death was dealt by the unerring shots of this noble little band. The enemy, with his large force, had come within 80 steps of us, when a hasty retreat down the hill with a circuitous route to the left saved us from the prisoner's cell.

Our loss was comparatively great. The men fought exceedingly well. Among the bravest, I deem it necessary to mention W. T. Rea, a private of Company K; Private E. G. Taylor, Company B, and Ensign L. R. Bowyer.

Loss in this engagement, 8; names* heretofore furnished.

B. BROWN
Captain, Commanding Regiment

---

*Not found.

[Indorsement.]

Brigadier-General GARNETT:

This regiment was acting more directly under your orders than those of its commander, Captain Brown, who was present during the engagement. I did not recognize Adjutant Wood as its commander on that day, he being only third lieutenant.

Respectfully,

JAMES D. McINTIRE

APPENDIX VI

FRAGMENTS OF ORIGINAL MANUSCRIPT OF REMINISCENCES OF BIG I

Note: The following narrative is all that is extant of the original draft of the Reminiscences. This draft, in Wood's own hand, is in possession of Miss Emma G. Wood of Charlottesville, Virginia, and was made available for publication through her kindness. The fragments, reproduced without any revision, are included, despite some repetition, to provide a sample of Wood's account as it first came from his pen and to present some good stories omitted from the published version.

On the 18th day July (Thursday) 1861 I left home to join the Monticello Guard (Co. A. 19th Va. Regt. infantry) Arriving at Manassas Junction on the evening of the same day and was greeted by the booming of the cannon on Bull Run about five miles distant, at Union Mills. This small engagement even at the distance mentioned was enough for me doubtless at that time as I have now some recollections of feeling "I would as soon be at home in Ch-ville." Spending the night at Manassas I marched with others—who like myself had been somewhat tardy in joining the Army—and found the Co. at Mitchells Ford on Bull Run on the 19th July. I became at once a C. S. Soldier, but was allowed to spend the remainder of the day visiting friends in Cos. A & B. On the 20th I was ordered by Capt. W. B. Mallory commanding Co. A to take my turn in throwing up Breastworks. Putting on a pr. of buck gloves I took my place with spade in hand to throw up dirt. All my life I had been weak, spare and sickly, and though twenty-one years of age, weighed only one hundred & twenty-seven pounds. My white shirt, standing collar and carefully arranged hair gave the boys a good target for good humoured jests which was as good humouredly received. That night I slept soundly with W. C. Payne under a pr. of nice white blankets in a tent. Hands had blistered and joints ached for I came to the army from behind the counter where my heaviest work had been handling rolls of cloth and putting up bundles of dry goods. Sunday morning, July 21st, I was awakened by the unearthly sound of a cannon which was supposed to be at the inconvenient distance of a mile. Dressing myself with haste I took my place in the trench with a Minnie musket in my hand. I had never drilled an hour, and the mysteries of loading in nine times & keeping step were things entirely unknown to me. There I was, however, a soldier only in the position occupied—in all else possibly the greenest of the awkward squad. After taking my position in line I remember wishing the Yankees would not try to cross at this ford, & I more than once thought of my unsoldierly appearance. I wore a brown frock coat and altogether wore nothing of the uniform except a cap. Some meat & bread were brought to us of which I partook heartily—not forgetting however to compare my breakfast with the Central Hotel fare from which I had so recently come. My next experience was an order "not to put your head above the works." This I conscientiously obeyed. My next experience was a sensation when Joe Slayton exclaimed—"Yonder they come Capt. Let me shoot, let me shoot for I can hit him." *One* Yank had appeared on the edge of the pines across Bull Run in our front hence the sensation. I obeyed orders & did not put my head above the works. Next experience was the fireing of a cannon of Lathams battery which was posted immediately on our left. Then came a report of the enemys long Tom, whose missile struck the hill some distance in our rear. Again Joe Slayton saw them coming and wanted to shoot—again I obeyed orders. Again and again Lathams battery sounded out in noise most terrible. Things were getting warm—musketry could be heard on our left, and soon a wounded man came from the left holding his torn hand and cursing the Yankees. The pines in our front—a small ps. of cleared land lay between us & them—was reported densely populated with Yankees at whom Gray Latham sent shot & shell in earnest. Latham finally became excited and called out "Capt Mallory! the battle of Waterloo was nothing" Again he exclaimed. "Ten pins is poor sport compared with this" "Don't let lazy Joe talk so much"—this in reference to the frequent shots from his gun a little to his (Lathams) left. He being at the ps. on the right. Just here—amid the roar of the musketry some distance to our left, the "talking" of lazy Joe just by us, and the belching of long Tom in our front Co A was called out of the trench and formed on the side of the hill in rear of our position. Freightened, yes freightened as much as any one could be, I took my position on the side of the hill, but was pleased to hear the command in a few minutes, "Return to your places in the trench" where I continued to obey orders. Just about this time our Col—Jno Bowie Strange called out his Sgt. Major. Joe Lipop—"Lipop I am without orders what shall I do"? Lipop replied—"Retreat to Manassas as speedily as possible" which advice however was not taken. We were again called out of the trenches and marched in the direction of the musketry on the left. Striking a Small branch we marched up its left bank and out of sight the Yanks as we thought, but we had not preceeded very far when a few stray bullets came from the direction of the enemy—One man of one of the Amherst Cos. was killed, and he was the first dead man I saw on the field of battle. About this time one of those Yankee balls struck Jack Collier of Co A. on the head making a small flesh wound. Volunteers to look after our wounded comrade were plentiful, one man, Jeff Mooney, declaring he had the very medicine for him. The very medicine proved to be a bottle of No. 6. Thirsty, Hot, Freightened we continued our march up the branch for two or three hundred yards, filed to the right through a small body of woods and formed in line in front of the Lewis House (I think) facing the Yankees. A Battery New Town unlimbered in our front and began rapidly to fire upon the foe. The fireing ceased, the smoke vanished and then the prettiest sight I ever saw was before us—the Yankees running with might and main towards the North. As they run a few shots from the battery in our front hurried them up the hill beyond the Run. Our regiment marched in pursuit, crossed Bull Run and made a detour to the left of the Pike. On this march I saw more knapsacks, blankets & Oil & Gum cloths piled up than I thought existed. We did not fire a gun but always said we were in the Battle of Bull Run.

Monday July 22nd, 1861 was a rainy day and our Co. was at its quarters at Lewis's ford. I got a permit to spend two hours on the field of battle, and for the first time saw numerous evidences of war's fearful havoc. The dead were numerous, but no where did I see so many as just east of the Henry house. I wandered over the grounds and when informed by an older soldier and more knowing comrade that this battle would secure our independance I rejoiced in the thought that no more scenes of carnage were to offend my vision and no more such suffering as the hospital displayed would curdle my blood. "Where ignorance is bliss" &c I returned to camp with a good overcoat, a splendid canteen, and a fair piece of oil cloth all of which were destined to be used in scenes more horrible than those just mentioned.

We remained at Lewis ford on the 23—but I think we moved to Cub Run on the 24th. Here I learned the manual of arms and to keep time in drill. In fact I became quite learned in the drill before another move. It was at Cub Run I think, that Wm Perley became distinguished as frog leg Perley. Not far from Camp was a nice pond of water and Perley hied away to its dam and banks and produced in camp the delicious frog legs of blessed memory. I may as well mention in passing that Carson Vandegrift was probably the loudest mouthed denunciator of Perley's bad taste, until by hook or crook he got a morsel of the delicious frog legs at any evenings repast—after which poor Perley's ingenuity was taxed in making excuses for not Supplying the said R. C. Vandegrift with all the frog legs his appetite craved.

About this time I was one morning detailed for guard duty and marched some distance from camp and posted near an old Virginia frame residence. By some means no instructions had been given me. I was simply told to walk that beat —from the corner of the garden to locust tree and bear myself like a Soldier. A path from the house to a spring in the bottom below crossed my beat. Pretty soon the walking became monotonous and my musket became heavy & I invented some new methods of carrying arms. In the midst of my attempts to improve on Hardee a middle aged gentleman of medium size, of dark or brown complexion, with piercing or cutting black eyes passed down the path. I observed simply his intent observation of my presence and soon forgot all about him. In twenty or thirty minutes he passed back to the house and this time I was very near the path. He said nothing and I said nothing, but immediately after he passed Liet. Jno C. Culin, the officer of the guard, came tearing at full speed and exclaimed "Sentinel! do you know what you have done"? I replied "I have done nothing but kill some grass along this beat that I am getting very tired of." "Why you have allowed Gen'l Beauregard to pass you without presenting arms." "Was that Gen'l Beauregard and what is presenting arms anyway." Whereupon right there and then, that efficient officer and accomplished drill master initiated me into the arts of saluting a Superior officer. My remissness was forgiven I suppose because the Genl had on no insignia of office. This was the first time I saw Gen'l Beauregard.

Not long after this I was on a detail for duty on the outpost and have some recollection of the terrible thought that probably no soldier was between me and the enemy. The Sgt.

of the outpost sent me to camp that evening for the counter-sign for the night. This was furnished me by Adjt. C. C. Wertenbaker, and I remember that I felt my importance as I wended my way back to the headquarters of the out post with the three cornered paper in which was folded the word "Madrid" which had been given to me orily also. The Sgt. was about to post the guard for the night and awaited my arrival for the word which I furnished him with a due sense of the issues involved in having the word correct. The Sgt. gave the sentinels the word as he left each at his post. Two hours rolled around and my time to go on post arrived. I relieved Wm F. Gordon of Co "B" and was much horrified when he said "Mr Wood are you the certain the word was given you Mad-rid, for the correct pronunciation of the word is Ma-drid." Thus I was left on out post for the first time at night with the great uncertainty of the countersign being correct. Imagine if you please how often I spelled the capital of Spain during my two hours, and wondered if it were possible that Wm F. Gordon knew more than all the officers at Head Quarters not excepting Jno. Bowie Strange and C C Wertenbaker.

My two hours passed away as did the other two hours of that night without an occasion for me to decide which was the proper pronunciation of the word. Our camp on Cub Run proving unhealthy we were moved to higher grounds nearer to Centreville. It was about this time that the Co. was ordered to prepare for a march or a fight. Knapsacks were hastily packed and haversacks filled and the commanding voice of Capt Mallory rang out—"fall in—fall in"—when Tip Collier came running to Capt Mallory with his champaign basket on his shoulder & some cooking utensils under his arm and exclaimed—"Captain what shall I do with my gun for I have more than I can carry." It was a false alarm however and we did not move though on dress parade a few evenings afterwards the Soldiers were informed that extra baggage must be sent to Manassas.

About this time Tom Randolph of Co "A" who was on Gen'l Cocke's staff was taken sick & found a comfortable home with a Mr Hays near camp. At his request W. C. Payne was instructed to report at Mr. Hays to attend Tom Randolp[h]. One day a stranger approached the Hays mansion and stopped to rest on the porch. He (the stranger) was dressed in a new con[federate] uniform and was evidently an inteligent gentleman. Entering into conversation with Payne he asked numerous questions about Ch-ville and the University, and finally that a cousin of his entered service from Ch-ville and he wished so much to ascertain his Co. & Regiment. He said his cousin's name was Tom Randolph of Mississippi for whom he cherished the warmest friendship. Payne replied Sir if you will walk with me to that door I will shew you a Tom Randolph of Mississippi who may prove to be the friend you mention. The surprised Stranger obeyed and when he beheld the sick, emaciated and fever tossed Randolph he suddenly stopped and burst into tears for this was none other than the cousin and friend for whom he had for months diligently enquired.

While in this encampment Joe Birckhead—known in the army as Beaury or Beauregard—was on camp guard, and Col. Strange conceived the idea of testing the watchfulness of the Sentry. Passing out at another portion of the camp he attempted to enter camp on Beaurys beat, but was stopped with that stentorian voice "Who comes there"? The reply "Col Strange *without* the countersign" was given. "Mark time Col. Strange—mark time. Corporal of the guard post No 4" called out the sentinal, and there the Col. had to *mark time* until the corporal arrived.

About this time I got a uniform, and upon running my

hand over my face discovered I had whiskers in prospect—
thus you see I was a man as well as a soldier.

We moved forward and pitched our tents north of Fairfax C. H. some time in—and here many incidents occurred
which might be of use to the Historian. Measles spread
through the army and Typhoid fever abounded. Mat Sales,
Joe Fuller of Co A. died and many were sick. Camp duty
became more irksome—false alarms numerous and heavy
picket duty on Masons and Munson Hills gave us exercise in
abundance. Who does not remember the "up the hill and down
again, and no blood spilled" "break ranks" of Col. Strange or
the "Attention my people! put on your stickers, them felloes
are a coming" of Col Preston of the 28th or the equaly original
command of Col Preston. "Fall in 28th—fall in," and then
raising his voice as he exclaimed "If you don't fall in, I will
march the regiment off and leave every one of you behind"

From Mason's hill I saw for the first time the capitol at
Washington. Here (at Masons hill) I for the first time, whilst
on picket at night, imagined the bushes in my front were the
enemy creeping upon us in the dim starlight, and more than
once leveled my gun to stop the approach, but fortunately
never fired and saw on the morrow the approaching enemy to
be only friendly sassafras & briars. Here I appropriated my
first roasting ears we found a late patch and indulged in the
sweets of somebody's peaches. One night I was detailed for
picket near Munsons hill. My post was north of the hill on a
path leading down an ivy thicket to a small stream, beyond
which imagination peopled the country with the enemy. The
night was dark, the ivy thicket was lonesome, the air chilly, no
fire was allowed and instructions very strict to remain at one
place and not move about, but listen and observe. It was my
second stand for the night when after being left alone I distinctly heard a noise as if some one was opening the bushes to
my right—then a twig broke not far from me and all was still

again. Pit a pat went my heart, great cold waves passed up the spinal cord, noiselessly I cocked my minnie, eagerly I bent forward to catch another sound which came again as a fox (I supposed) trotted off to the rear. I certainly did not sleep on post that night. This post was near the spot where Billy Payne and C C Wertenbaker had a friendly chat with the enemy mid way between the lines, from which friendly confab they returned through an old mill which just at that time was visited by one of our cavalrymen who was in search of extra rations for his horse. As Payne came in from the Yankee side of the mill the Cavalryman cocked his pistol and came near sending a bullet through the body of the intruder. Fortunately each recognised the other to be a friend. Very soon after this our friend Payne was taken with the fever which left him almost blind and thus deprived the C. S. of a good and true soldier.

Our lines were drawn in and these posts abandoned. Winter approached and to the other objections to picket duty came cold & Longer nights. I remember being on picket near Germantown or what we called germantown. My post was on a main road leading northward. The night was very dark, and rain and sleet added to my discomfort. I had become very cold and was rejoicing to see that it was day, but lo, in the dim light of the morning I could see horseback riders approaching from the enemys direction. Sgt. Pig. Huffman (Alex, was his name) joined me at this time—just as three cavalrymen came in hailing distance. Proper signals were given and the riders passed into our lines. One of them stopped however to have a friendly chat with Huffman. Presently he moved on and Huffman turning to me remarked "I wonder what that trifling fellow stopped to talk with me for." "Who is he Pig"? "Why that poor wretch Jack Mosby," and this was the first time during the war that I heard the name called of one whose exploits filled the world with amazement.

About this time Geo. Watson Carr was appointed Colonel

of the 19th—Col. Strange remaining as he had been Lt. Col.
There was considerable red tape about Co. Carr—for instance
—when our assistant regimental commissary P. Jacheri rode up
to Col. Carr's tent on some matter of business connected with
the commissary department the col asked "Who are you sir"?
"I am P. Jacheri commissary of the 19th Va Regt." "Get down
sir—get down off that horse"—and P. Jacheri rolled down
and approached the col in a manner more in keeping with
military discipline We got the laugh on Col. Carr a few days
after on the occasion of a division review on which occasion
we were to pass in review before Prince Polniac. The Regt.
had been formed, and was at an "order arms." Col. Carr at
regulation distance in front was reading the order of exercises
which was concealed in his hat—the hat being in his hand—
when time came for the Regt. to present arms. "Present Arms!"
came the order but not a hand moved. Astonished beyond
measure and turning redder in the face than was natural the
Col. had recourse to his hat & said aloud "Lo! what a grave
error I have committed" "Shoulder arms." "Present arms" and
then all went in usual form & harmony. I remember Dagan
bringing me a nice ps. of shoat and upon being questioned
where he struck it, replied "I lets no pig bite me" and no more
questions were asked [by] me. Winter had come—we had
moved back to Centreville and went into winter quarters. Each
mess built a shanty with stick chimney & large fire place. Our
mess consisted of R. C. Vandegrift, Thos G Wertenbaker,
James Perley, Joe Birckhead, Geo. Thomas Johnson, James
Brown, W. T. Jones & W. N. Wood all of whom are now
living except the lamented Wertenbaker—Feby 1873 This
was Mess No 1, but was dubbed the Methodist Camp Meeting
Mess, because they had regular family prayers before retiring
at night. I was relieved of camp duty by being appointed clerk
to Adjt. C. C. Wertenbaker, but stuck to my mess. I recall many
ludicrous incidents, but one of the best had escaped me until

recently reminded of it. Jno Hill, Wm Cloa, Buck Baily, Wm. Vaughan & Jno Dodd had been confined in the guard house for some trivial offense, and Capt. Mallory got permission from the Col. to have them get wood [for] his (the Capt's) Mess. The boys went at it with a will and soon a good pile of wood appeared at the Capt's door, but to the Captains disgust, upon investigation he found every stick was black gum—a wood that will not burn well and is extremely difficult to split. —The joke was turned on the boys however when they were ordered to return to the captains shanty and split that wood. At it they went however and after due exercise begged the privilege of returning to the forest and getting some good wood—which they did. It was whilst in these winter quarters that Teltow—the leader of the band imbibed freely of apple jack and concluded that things were not fixed right in camp. "For instance," said Teltow, "the leader of the band is one of the most important characters of Regiment and should be so recognized on the Pay Roll" He finally said he would go and see Col. Strange—who was in command of the Regiment at that time—about it. His messmates tried to pursuade him not to do so but to no effect. He promised however not to do or say anything that the "col could take hold of" but would "talk sarcastically to the col." He staggered to the col's quarters and pulled aside the tent flap that was serving for a door and poking his head in exclaimed—"Strange you are a damned old louse." "Take that man to the guard house" was the reply and thus the leader of the band became an inmate of those undesirable quarters. The camp meeting mess had a few books, a set of chess men, and took one Richmond paper which was read aloud and thus the time was pleasantly occupied. I remember one occasion when Jim Perley got the paper. I was busy making up light bread & the others variously employed— "A fight at Dranesville" read Jim. "What result" some one exclaimed. Jim thinking about particulars of the engagement

—which by the way were not given—replied "No result at all —we whipped 'em"—and this joke has followed James Perley to the present time.

The winter passed by and in February I recd a reenlisted furlough of thirty days, and my first visit home as a soldier was enjoyed.

Returning to my command I met the boys in Orange Co. on their way to the Peninsular. Spending a few days in orange our march to Yorktown commenced one muddy, rainy Snowy day in the latter part of March 1862, encamping that night near Louisa C. H. In such a wretched condition were the roads that our commissary wagons failed to come up—and after Maj. H. W. Jones had secured some flour for us our only means of cooking supper was by heating rocks and putting a hoecake thereon and setting them—the rocks—before the fire. I also tried the experiment of winding the dough around a dogwood stick—scraped nicely—and turning it before the fire until done. We marched to Richmond and took boats for the Peninsular. Here the army was reorganized and the different companies elected officers—After six ballots Jno. C. Culin was elected capt.—defeating C. C. Wertenbaker by one vote. I was elected Jr. second lieuetnant, and was at once appointed Acting Adjutant, and entered at once upon the duties, but retaining my place in the mess. On the evening of May 3d our Regiment broke camp and started towards Richmond. We passed Genl J E B Stuart who jocularly remarked—"It is Strange—passing strange" just as the regiment with Col. J B Strange at the head passed him. On the 4th of May we arrived in the immediate vicinity of Williamsburg. A large detail had been made from the regiment to go with the train of wagons, with Jas Perley at the head of it. Wm. Turner Jones was also detailed on this duty, but saying he did not care to be pushing wagons out of the mire Jeff Mooney took his place. Our wagon not coming up our prospects for supper were slim. Jones (W. T.) prepared our bed (which was simply spreading an oil cloth on the ground and unfolding a blanket to pull over us) and retired supperless. Before I joined him however the wagon containing flour & cooking utensils came up, and I went to Jones and informed him now was our time to cook something for immediate use and for the next day. Being sufficiently awake to understand what I meant he grunted out—"All right anything you do will be satisfactory to me" and turned over and went to sleep. After cooking a lot of nice biscuit and enjoying a cup of genuine coffee I joined Jones which has, thus far in life, proved to be the last time we bunked together. The next day—May 5th—was damp and cool The regiment was formed about ten oclock (a.m.) and we marched into Williamsburg from the North West. There met us as we entered the old town the report of musketry & artillery—in fact everything indicated a battle in progress. The command was given —"In place—rest." however & for some time it seemed we were not to be in the engagement. Col. Strange's peculiar "Attention." put another aspect upon affairs, and we headed towards the noise of battle—leaving Port Magruder to our left we had to [march] over [a] clear stretch of about one hundred yards which seemed to be ploughed by the enemys artillery. The boys began to dodge the bullets and were reproved by Col. Strange who rode as if on a turkey hunt. When in the midst of the "clear stretch" shells were flying uncomfortably near and Col Strange "ducked" his head which caused some of the boys to laugh. "You can dodge the big ones but never mind the little ones," called out the Col. "Double quick" and soon we were beyond the point of *immediate* danger. At the edge of cleared field we formed a line of battle and advanced through a piece of woods until we came to the fallen trees which Magruder had cleared in front of Fort Magruder. Here we halted within about one hundred yards of a Yankee battery over which the Star Spangled banner proudly waved. Some protected by the fallen timber and some by the standing trees we commenced fireing. Standing near Col. Strange I saw a well dressed officer approach him, and heard him say "Col Strange! take two companies from the right of your regiment and charge that battery." I almost if not quite trembled for one of those companies was "A." I was greatly relieved however when Col. Strange replied—"Gen'l Hill, I do not recognise your authority as Gen'l Pickett is on the ground." About this time W. T. Jones received his wound—a ball passing through his face. We thought he was killed. In a few minutes Gen'l Pickett ordered a charge. Col Strange sent me to the left of regiment with the instructions—Pell Mell we went—over big trees and little trees—as they lay in our way—over bushes & stumps & over dead Yankees & wounded Yankees—many of the wounded crying upon the Lord for mercy, and not a few exclaiming "I surrender—I surrender" On we went until we reached the battery—Alex (Pig) Huffman leading around the battery on the east and Tom Randolph leading on the west—Randolph & Huffman meeting on the enemys side of the gun shook hands and yelled louder than before—In a minute Alex Huffman fell dead from a long range gun of the enemy. Thus Co "A's" first death in battle was one of the bravest of the land. The wounded were numerous, but all recovered— though W. T. Jones was never again acceptable for duty. Jumping upon one of the captured horses Col. Strange rode off to announce his capture. I reformed the regiment (as adjt) and soon the gallant Col. marched us off the field towards Williamsburg & halted near Fort Magruder at "In place rest." A cool wind sprang up and all of us suffered with cold. Gen'l Pickett rode up and requested the use of his adjutant and I was ordered to report. I was informed by Gen'l Pickett that he had lost sight of the 28th Va Regt. and did not know where it was, and ordered me to go in search of it—instructing me to leave the battle field to my left and strike the woods near where we formed our line of battle. Off I went on horseback, down a bottom with a small branch on my left. Said branch soon deepened into an immense gulley and yet I must cross it. Continueing down the ditch I came to a bridge made of small round poles & I attempted to cross. The poles commenced to roll and the next thing I knew my horse was suspended on the poles—all four feet having gone through between the poles. I dismounted & wondered how I could get the horse out of its awkward position. I began to remove the poles—thinking it possible that I could drop the horse into the ditch. He commenced exerting himself however and soon landed safely on the right side of the gulley. Mounted again off I went in search of the 28th which I came up with just in time as they were going straight towards the enemy and would soon [have] been butchered or captured. We spent the night south east of Williamsburg and next morning very early passed through the town on our way towards Richmond. Mud—Mud—Mud—the deepest I ever saw and the most of it. On the 6th whilst halted on the road Gen'l Jos E. Johnston passed us and as the boys gave him a rousing cheer he exclaimed—"That sounds better to me today than it did to the enemy on yesterday" which brought a louder cheer still. Thomas Grady Wertenbaker left us a few days afterwards never to return. He died in June (the 23d) at his home. A noble young man—brave—modest—generous & pious he passed doubtless to a better & brighter world. Those who were severely wounded (of Co A) at Williamsburg [and] fell in the enemies hands were W. T. Jones already mentioned —Jno D. Durrett & C W Vandegrift.

Wm Culin, A. J. Brown, J. J. Christian, W. N. Johnson, M. W. Wingfield & W W Maury were wounded but were brought away—Nine wounded & one killed. The next twenty (20) days were employed in routine duty in camp at several different places and no incident is remembered worthy of note. The regiment was encamped near bottoms bridge and then nearer Richmond. Drilling and building breastworks were the general occupations. About the 26th May we changed locations—moving to a point more nearly north of the city and something further from it. On the night of Thursday May 29th 1862 we were drenched with a severe rain and I recall the extreme unpleasantness of the occasion as I had no tent. On Friday the 30th extra rations were prepared in obedience to orders and early Saturday morning the regiment took up a line of march eastward. Later in the day everything indicated a fight—fireing in front—orderlies riding rapidly —generals looking solemn & company and regimental officers very strict. We halted for the night not far from Seven Pines and learned that a big fight had taken place and we were "not in it." We had halted in a swamp and in order not to sleep in the water I cut off or broke off tops of small pines and piled them until I had a superb bed in the midst of mud and muck. I ate cold rations as it was difficult to find a place dry enough to make a fire or wood dry enough to burn. Sunday morning June 1st dawned upon us clear and warm. The regiment was formed by or before eight oclock and marched to the battlefield of the previous day. Arms were stacked in the road and the men disposed of themselves pretty much as they wished. Some of tents of the enemy had been left standing, & numerous arbors—formed by cutting bushes and resting them upon poles supported by forks stuck in the ground— invited the forager and curiosity hunter to investigation. Many a trinket was picked up, boxes of crackers, packages of coffee sugar &c were found. The boys were having a regular pick- nick this beautiful sabbath morning. I was standing near the head of the stacked arms looking yankeewards when suddenly puffs of smoke rose from the bushes about three hundred yards in front, followed by the report of musketry, whilst here

and there the thud of bullets against stumps and the few standing trees were heard. The Col. exclaimed "Adjt. form the
regiment," and I called out "fall in fall in" and in a few
minutes a body of well drilled soldiers was marching towards
the bushes from whence came the shots that put an end to the
foraging. Gen'l Pickett rode up—the column was halted and
dressed in line and the word "forward March" given. "Don't
fire until you see them." "Steady boys steady." and similar
expressions were freely used. On [we] went over fallen
timbers—through sharpened pine limbs arbattis, and halted
on the edge of an immense frog pond. "By the left flank" and
we marched about two hundred yards and still no enemy had
been seen. "Halt,"—"front"—"Forward" came the commands
& again—"Halt" "lie down." We were in the woods now and
our time for action had nearly arrived. I was standing near
the centre of the regiment, a little in the rear when casting my
eyes to the left about two hundred yards I saw a body of the
enemy in line of battle marching to our rear. I reported this
to Col. Strange who said they must be our men and ordered
me to have our colors displayed. I stepped back in plain view
and fastened my eyes upon U. S. flag and knew they were the
enemy. Approaching the colonel to inform him of my cer-
tainty as their being the enemy I observed through the dense
undergrowth in our front here a blue coat approaching—when
lo! our boys let fly the missiles of death and received in return
one of the most deadliest fires the 19th ever received and at as
short range—Quick and lively was the fireing and away went
the enemy to his breastworks not far off. We remained on the
ground long enough to get our dear & wounded and then
retired—The dead of Co A. were James Jones, Marion Pierce,
James Collier, William Kidd

*   *   *   *

Arriving at Gordonsville by rail on the 13th of August
we encamped in Louisa County near Bowler's Mill. On our

way from Gordonsville to this camp we passed the camp of the 7th Va regiment in which was a company from Green county containing numerous friends of the writer. One of them hailed me and asked me to dine with him—adding "just got a box from home—so come on." This was a temptation not to be resisted. And what a box it was. Fried chicken, old ham, apple pies &c &c. "Here try this before you begin"—"No thank you I never drink" was the reply as a canteen was handed over. "It's nothing but innocent cherry bounce—why it wouldn't hurt a baby," with which assurance a good hearty pull was taken from the canteen. It was good—in fact so very palatable was this cherry bounce that a second hearty pull was taken before the box was tackled. Reader if you wish to enjoy a meal, get real hungry and then find a box from a homestead in Green County. Eating and talking consumed half an hour and Big i arose to go—or rather *tried to,* for somehow the trees seemed to be dancing, and the men around the box terribly mixed up, the tongue was thick, the knees weak, the head whirling, and the leafy shade inviting, all because cherry bounce was innocent. "All present or accounted for" at roll call that evening. This encampment near Bowler's Mill though of short duration was one of the most pleasant now recalled. Short and sweet was the stay however as we struck tents and bid them a long farewell on or about the 17th August and went in search of the boastful Pope. Marching northward we crossed the Rapidan passed through the Eastern portion of Culpeper. In the vicinity of Stephensburg a spy was caught and hung. As we approached the Rappahannock river, the enemy opened upon us with long range artillery, and a shell burst very near a part of Co A engaged in playing poker under a blanket supported by a musket at each corner, making a shade just large enough to accommodate a poker party.

*   *   *   *

We are in the bottom, and up cemetary hill we start, Grape and canister scour the ground. Down, down go the boys. The remainder press forward. The wall (stone & dirt), the enemys breatworks just in front. Suddenly the firing ceases in our front, and the brave boys make renewed efforts to reach the goal. Just then—when within twenty yards of the rock fence, I receive a blow on the right leg. Am I wounded? Leaning against a rock I ascertain that it is only a bruise and forward again with the small remnant. I stop at the fence and looking to the right and left, I feel that we are disgraced, where are the men who started in the charge? With one single exception I had witnessed no cowardice, and yet they are not here. A thin skirmish line only remain. Continueing to survey the scene I observe to our right a colum of the enemy forming a line of battle on *our* side of the fence. Their right is at the fence, their left extends into the field behind us. To remain means life in prison. To retreat means probable death but possibly, safety in our lines; and without a moments hesitation I turned my back to the fence and started across that three quarters of a mile, over which we had so recently come. I was tired and thirsty, and limping down the hill I felt like taking shelter behind a pile of rails that lay inviting in my way but did not do so. The enemy opened upon us again. I increased my speed somewhat. Suddenly a twinge in the side, and a ball of the wadding from my coat & vest in front caused me to slacken my speed to a slow walk. All along this retreat, I had abundant evidence, in the dead and wounded, that we were not disgraced. At last I passed over the hill & hasted to the shade, where I found an number of wounded who had preceeded me. The first voice I heard was Lucian Jones who asked if I were wounded. I replied Yes and asked after his wounds. He replied, "I am mortally wounded, but I fell in the discharge of duty and near the cannons mouth"

With a view of investigating my wound I pulled off my

coat and found it much torn on right side by the bullet. My vest was also torn on same side. But as yet nothing had shown stains of blood. With intense anxiety and bated breath, I removed my shirt and found that torn by the same ball and on it a small blood stain. Further investigation relieved the mind, for the ball had done less damage than I have frequently received from briars though more painful. By the time I was dressed, I saw Genl. Pickett approaching with tears streaming down his cheek. He extended his hand in silence but as he rode off half sobbed "My brave men, my brave men."

All who were able to do so,—except those attending the wounded—took position in line with face turned to the foe. The men were easily rallied, and there was not much confusion. The extent of our disaster was a matter of conjecture. We had failed for the first time to do what we tried to do, but the earnestness of the effort was attested by the great loss sustained. Our brigade commander Gen. R. B. Garnett was killed. This was indeed a great loss, for I verily believe his superior as a brigade commander was not in the army. So much did I admire him that my youngest child bears his name. The Col. of our regiment was wounded. The Lt. Col. killed as mentioned. The major—gallant Charley Peyton—escaped with a slight wound. The Acting Adjutant—James D. McIntire

* * * *

Our approach to each other was slow, when he descending a small hill near the old Campbell residence was lost to sight. I embraced this opportunity to get over the high stake fence on my right, and was not sorry to see him riding at full speed towards Mayos shop—having turned about in the bottom. I now knew a raiding party was at hand, and in order to ascertain more definitely as to number and movements I hurried through the woods to the Rio road, & arrived near the stone culvert, in time to ascertain that the command was large, and marching towards the town of Charlottesville. Hurrying home I joined Jas H Bumley just as his plowman—John Southall who now lives near Hydraulic—came riding up exclaiming— "The soldiers have taken my horses." "What horses?" "John Rattler and—" John Southall told me a few days since that John Rattler was the best horse the county ever produced.

J H B. had his remaining horses (about fifteen) hurried through a gate way, and over the barn hill and concealed in the clifts, and with many of his servants. (He owned about one hundred) I joined the crowd on the barn hill, and seeing a single cavalryman approaching the residence of my father, remarked, if I had a horse I would pay my respects to the visitor. A Mr. Ellis standing near replied "There is my horse— Mount," and mount I did, and galloped down the hill, through Mr. B's stable lot, and up the hill towards the house mentioned. As I passe near Mr B's house I observed his school teacher—Miss Chancllor—standing on the porch, and as I approached my fathers residence my only sister beckoned to me to go back. She saw the crowded road and knew who they were. I saw the lone horseman as he rode from one end of the yard to the other watching my zigzag approach. Finally we faced each other—divided by the yard. I raised my carbine and he leveled his pistol and just then the crowd in the road —about two hundred yards distance—fired upon me, causing my horse to jump just as I fired. My opponent wheeled and ran and I did the same. I had not gone far however when I discovered my horse was weakening and I could not hurry. I went through the same gateway & started up the barnhill— my horse having come to a walk. A squadron of the enemy had left the main road and came at a charge down the road leading to Mr. B's residence. My safety was in bravado, so waving my cap to them halloed at the top of my voice "Come ahead" They stopped at the gate and seemed to count the tracks of the horses that had recently passed through, and then

rode on to residence of J H B rode in the yard and one of
them asked who it was that sent that bullet through his clothes.
They departed quickly, doing no damage not even getting
down.

Upon returning to camp from my short stay at home on
furlough, I found the regiment on a bleak hill side with the
March winds blowing the smoke in every direction. They had
been called out to protect the city from the Dahlgreen raiders,
who managed to get off without coming in contact with the
19th. Returning to the snug quarters on Chafins farm we spent
some time in quiet repose. Thus the month of March passed
off and April came. During the month of April we made a few
hurried trips to different places—to add strength to weak
points, but without coming in contact with the enemy. The
month of May was ushered in with all sorts of rumors as to
the movements of the enemy. We had become so proud of
our Gettysburg glory that we were content to hold the important point of Chafins farm to the end of the chapter. One
bright morning in early May, probably the 8th, we received
orders for light marching preparations. Everything was sent
to Richmond except such articles usually taken in action. We
skirted around Richmond — on the North side, — and
bivouacked that night near the brooke turnpike. On the 9th
we marched a little eastward, then a little westward and
before night northward. Rain began to fall and the May
nights were chilly. On the 10th we hurried in the direction of
Yellow Tavern and soon heard the old familiar sound of
artillery. Entering a piece of woods at a double quick, we
were saluted by shells from an unseen foe. A shell passed
through the woods and burst almost in the midst of Co A as
we hurried along, but did no damage except throwing mud
and water upon a number of the men. We had not the opportunity of engaging the enemy,—the entire fight being that of
cavalry. General Stuart fell in this fight, and many a cavalry-

man fought his last battle on this memorable day. We expected to be hurried to the front, for news from the Wilderness reached us. Picketts division rejoined the army of Northern Va late in May and thus became united again On the morning of May 26th 1864 our regiment was aroused about day break and marched to the outside line of defences not far from Hanover junction, and immediately took position in the breast-works. All day we expected an attack but it was not made. Late in the evening of that day the writer was detailed for outpost duty with this remark. "The detail for the night has been made with the exception of two men. You are instructed to select from the 19th two of its best men to be stationed at an angle of great importance." I selected Lon Lane and Joe Points of Co "A." than whom better soldiers nor braver spirits ever shouldered a musket. To this important angle we were conducted in the dark and there spent one of the longest (seemingly) and most quiet nights of the war. The worst of it was, we had to lie prostrate all night peeping over a small mound of dirt, and expecting every minute to hear and see the enemy approaching. On the morning of the 29th we returned to the lines, but the constant expectation of an attack forbade sleep. We expected sleep that night, but when night came, we were constantly extending our line to the right and there was no sleep. This was the time when Grant, becoming satisfied that he could not break through Lee's line, had hurried to his left, expecting to find an easy and short road to Richmond from Cold Harbor. Lee extended his right so rapidly that on every occasion the wily foe found himself confronted by the boys in grey. Excuse me, I am not writing history, but personal reminiscences.

On the evening of June 1st heavy firing on our right admonished us of new efforts to break through our lines. Leaving the line of defence we double quicked to the right through a wooded country up a branch and about dark took position on a hill in a broomsedge field dotted over with old field pines. Here we were shelled for about an hour with no opportunity to return the punishment in kind. Later in the night we advanced directly toward the enemy and found protection behind some old works that were used doubtless in 1862. The night wore away

The third day of June 1864 was a cloudy damp day. Early in the morning the 19th regiment took position in the woods in line of battle with considerable space between the companies,—thus covering more space than usual in an engagement. The centre of the regiment—Co K—was thrown forward a short distance and hence more exposed when the attack came, for which we had not long to wait. The heavy mass of infantry was thrown against our works on our immediate left several times, and every time left the ground well spotted with blue as they sought safety beyond the reach of musketry. But in front of the 19th, a column of infantry advanced within fifty yards of the centre of the regiment and took position behind the trees, and held their position during the sixty minutes that the battle lasted. Late in the action I received word to take command of Co K as all the officers of that company had been killed. Capt Culin of A. had been wounded and leaving the company in command of Sgt. James Perley I went to K. and the company almost annihilated. Wm. T Rea and a few others remained but the bulk of the company was either killed or wounded. The enemy left our front about this time and the battle was over. And here more than on any other occasion the best and bravest had been killed. Our Sergeant Major Luther Wolf was killed—a man without fear and wellnigh recklessly brave. Lieut Robertson of Co. K was killed, in whom the regiment lost one of her best officers. Lt Evens of Company C was also a victim of the hours action, and many others. Capt Linthecum a Maryland Methodist minister who was acting as aid to Gen'l Pickett on this occasion was killed. The great loss to the regiment was James G. Woodson captain of Company K. who as Sr. captain was in command of the regiment. J. G. Woodson was a modest, quiet Christian gentleman with a high sense of honor and a great regard for duty. No ordeal, however trying; no service however irksome would he hesitate to dare and do if in the line of duty. The day he was killed he ought to have been in the hospital. Having lost a toe at Gettysburg he walked badly, and was almost too weak from sickness to travel. The surgeon and personal friends urged him to remain in the rear; but no! the colonel was absent and the command devolved upon him, and where duty pointed he tried to follow.

The list of casualties as published in the Examiner the next day, mentioned Capt. J. G. Woodson acting Major killed. Soon after the arrival of John McKennie with the mail & papers on the 5th of June—squads of men could be seen throughout the regiment, regardless of companies, discussing the list of casualties. Towards noon an indignation meeting was held and in one of the Richmond dailies on the 6th or 7th the following card appeared. In justice to the memory of Capt. James G. Woodson of Co. K 19th Va Regt. we wish to state that when he was killed on the 3d inst. he was in command of the regiment

Signed R. J. Holland—Capt. Co. D.
C. S. Irvine—Capt. Co. C.
W. N. Wood—Lieut. Co. A.

This plain statement of facts gave rise to some hard feelings and was the cause of trouble to the one whose name appears last among the signers of the card. He wrote it and so informed the colonel when questioned on the subject.

Gen'l Grant seems to have become satisfied after the second battle of cold harbor of his inability to whip the army of Northern Virginia, and made no further efforts in that

direction for some times. In fact it would seem that an idea
of strategy entered his brain, and he even dared to try to out
general our glorious Lee. In this he made an ignoble failure,
for when he crossed to the South side of the James and made
an advance the first troops in his way were those of Picketts
division who met the advance of the enemy on the pike
between Richmond and Petersburg. Our regiment marching
leisurely along the pike above mentioned arrived at a point
nearly opposite Chester on the railroad when a halt was made
and there seemed to be some confusion in front. "Lieut. deploy
your company as skirmishers and advance in the woods" was
the order I received. We quickly deployed and rapidly
advanced. For a distance of two hundred yards our advance
was not disputed, but upon emerging from the woods into a
small field a line of rifle pits appeared in the edge of the
woods beyond, and stooping down to examine an old barn
in the field which was rested on 2 ft. sawed blocks of wood,
we distincly saw the blue pants of the enemy behind the barn.
Company A had been joined by Company C. Capt Chas Irvine
commanding and we had then a good skirmish line. Sending
a flanking party to the right and left, and raising a yell, the
line advanced at a double quick, but the blue pants left before
our arrival and the last we saw of them they disappeared in
the woods beyond. We halted our line and sent a courier back
to ask for instruction. Our courier did not return quick enough
for us and the skirmish line was again advanced through the
woods a wide opening in front was discovered which when
approached proved to be the Howlett line which was vacated
by our troops when they hurried to the defense of Petersburg.
Still without instructions we for a moment hesitated, but pre-
suming the brigade was following in our tracks we decided
to make a bold dash for the works, which we did, at a double
quick yelling like mad! The works were abandoned by the
enemy without a shot and we took possession without the loss

of a single man. It was now nearly night and still no aid had come to the skirmish line. Dispatching a messenger to the command, we deployed so as to cover as much space as possible, put out videtts and then began a waiting for the brigade or instructions which lasted through the night. Every man on the thin line was a sentinel that night, and every man seemed to realize our peril and expect an attack. The writer walked from one end of our line to the other several times during the night and listened most anxiously for aid from the rear and most fearfully for the enemys tread in front. Neither came, & when the dawn of day appeared we saw no one in front or rear. About sun up however the brigade arrived and we took position on the Howlett line where we were destined to see service for many months.

* * * *

As fighting was the order of the day and not wishing to have more than one battle in each paper turn backward and insert a few incidents that have been omitted.

On our retreat from Centreville in March 1862 as the army passed a farm, there was sitting on the fence, in appearance, a regular "greeny" of a young man. Now was John Dodd's chance, for he was always in for fun, who looking up at the lank lazy looking young man on the fence asked "when are you going to jine the Army"? Quick as a flash came the reply.—"When you fellows stop running" and the laugh was on Dodd, who by the way was known in camp as Duff Green because of a resemblance he bore to a then resident of the Ridge.

* * * *

It was known that there was a still house about ten miles from camp. The night of Christmas eve was bright and clear. The moon shine inviting to ramblers, and a touch of the "creature" stimulating their desires. Six members of Co. A left camp quite early and passing themselves off as a guard in search of stragglers. About eleven oclock at night they arrived at a good looking farm house and asked for accommodations for the night. They were invited in a neat well furnished parlor to await their mid-night meal. They were soon invited to supper, but so great was their admiration of the pictures on the wall that the front man failed to observe the dining room was two steps lower than the parlor, consequently he pitched forward in a heavy fall, just missed the table, and rammed his head against the wall. Quiet restored they took seats at the table, when B. leaning back with dignity (and weight) broke the chairback, and throwing up his feet brought table and contents to the floor with him. They got something to eat at last and spent the night. Early next morning they found Beasley's still house, but *it was not in operation*. An interview of the proprietor resulted in filling a few canteens, which it was agreed should not be touched until camp was reached. Starting campward they soon came to a spring, and it was suggested that just one little pull would do no harm, so one canteen was unstopped and passed around and corked for camp but soon crossing a branch it was suggested they could take just a little and then hurry back. The suggestion was adopted, except the "just a little" and the canteens were lightened considerably. The barriers were gone, promises forgotten and neither spring nor branch was necessary for the uncorking process. Spying a small residence not far off hither they went to engage dinner. Whilst waiting for dinner a game of seven up was arranged and entered into as well as circumstances would admit. Two looks on made side bets, about which there was some misunderstanding, a fight ensued, the table was knocked over and the head of one of crowd butted against the back of the fire place. Peace restored, the table reset and all hands sat down to dinner. The [last] difficulty was referred to and the fight broke [out] afresh—table ware smashed, chairs broken, and

INDEX

INDEX

Albermarle County, Virginia, x
Allen, Pvt. James A., 92
Anderson's, 41
Anderson's Crossing, 58
Antietam Creek, 38, 39
Armistead's Brigade, 46
Army of Northern Virginia, xvi, xxvii, 40, 49, 58, 65, 129

Bacon, D. W. (M.), 92, 98
Bacon, W. O., 92, 98
Bailey, Buck, 10, 115
Bailey, G. W., 92
Bailey, Dr. R. G., 92
Bailey, Sgt. R. W., 92
Baldwin, J. W., 97
Baltimore & Ohio Railroad, 34
Batchellor, J. C., 93
Beasley's Still House, 132
Beauregard, General, xi, 6, 7, 109
Berryville, 41
Birckhead, James F., 88, 96
Birckhead, Joseph F. "Beaury," xi, 7, 10, 90, 93, 98, 111, 114
Birckhead, N. F., 96
Blue Ridge, 35, 41
Boonsboro (Boonsborough), xiv, 35, 36, 37, 102
Bowcock, W. H., 53
Bowen, Jno. A., 48, 90, 96, 98
Bowler's Mill, 27, 121, 122
Bowman, Jos. H., 93
Bowyer, Ensign L. R., 103
Boyd, Major, 60, 74
Brook Turnpike, 58
Brooks, A. J., 96, 98
Brown, Capt. B., xiv, 103
Brown, A. J., 90, 96, 98, 119
Brown, Jas. J., 10, 93, 98, 114
Brown, J. M. (One-arm), 36
Brown, W. A., 93
Brown, W. H., 90
Buck, Sgt. James R., 48, 90, 92, 98
Bull Run, 1, 2, 33, 78, 105, 106, 108
Bullock, Nannie (Wood's wife), xix
Bumley, Jas. H., 125
Bunker Hill, 49
Burkhead, J. G., 90, 98
Burkhead, N. F. (See Birckhead), 90, 98
Burnley, James H., 54
Burnley, Mr., 88

"Camp Meeting Mess" (Mess No. 1), xx, 10, 114
Campbell House, 54, 124
Carr, Colonel George Watson, xxii, 114
Cemetery Hill, 43, 46
Cemetery Ridge, ix, xvi
Centreville, 10, 83, 110, 114, 131
Chaffin's Farm, xvii, 52, 57, 58, 126
Chambersburg, Pa., 42
Chancellorsville, xvi
Charlottesville, x, xiv, 1, 53, 54, 125
Chester, 70
Chickahominy, 12, 22, 25
Chinn House, 4, 78, 79
Christian, J. J., 36, 93, 119
Clark, W. D., 93
Clicks, Wm., 97
Cloar, Jas. L., 93
Cloar, Jno. W., 93
Cloar, William J. (Cloa), 10, 90, 93, 99, 115
Cochran, Capt. John L., 103
Cold Harbor, 59, 63, 127
Cold Harbor (Second), xvii
Collier, H. H., 93
Collier, Jack, 3, 107
Collier, James, 19, 93, 121
Collier, J. W. H., 93, 98
Collier, Tip, 7, 110
Conrad House, 78
Copeland, N. F., 96
Crank Road, 53
Crigler, Mr., 84
Cub Run, xxiii, 6, 8, 108, 110
Culin, Geo. W., 93
Culin, Capt. John C., xxi, xxvii, 6, 11, 48, 64, 65, 72, 90, 92, 109, 116, 128
Culin, William, 13, 26, 93, 119
Culpeper, 41, 86, 122
Culpeper Courthouse, 27, 52

Dade, Lieut. Henry F. (Sgt.), 7, 90, 92
Dahlgren Raiders, 57, 126
Dagon, Comrade, xxii, 114
Deering, Capt., 32
Deering, Colonel, 44
Degan, Henry, 93
Dennis, Jno. M., 96, 98
Dobbins, R. L., 93, 98
Dodd, John, 10, 93, 98, 115, 131
Dranesville, 115

135

Date Due

FEB 2 5 '60			
MAR 1 0 '60			
MAR 7 '62			
APR 4			
MAY 1 3 '62			
OCT 1 0 '62			
	PRINTED	IN U. S. A.